"For twelve years I had the privilege of being a chaplain at a nursing home. I was never able to find the "right" book of prayers or rituals to assist the elderly in responding to their deep spiritual hungers. Now such a resource is available in Sr. Sandra DeGidio's *Prayer Services for the Elderly*. Pastoral ministers, volunteers in pastoral care work and families members of the elderly will find in this simple and direct text a helpful resource."

†Robert F. Morneau
Auxiliary Bishop of Green Bay

"I am very enthusiastic about the book because it meets a real need in a very helpful way. Sandra DiGidio is right about the importance of ritual in the lives of older persons, but I know of few resources available for those who minister to them. One can always write one's own services, of course, but this book will be a very valuable resource for those who are too busy to do so or who are not particularly liturgically minded.

"Sr. Sandra has created appropriate, useful liturgies that can be easily adapted to one's particular setting. Her experience with 'Third Agers' and compassion for them shine through in the sensitivity with which she has crafted these services. I especially appreciated the services for 'special occasions' because all too often these very important events pass largely unnoticed in long-term-care facilities, and they should not. Perhaps with such a useful resource at hand, we will all do a better job of marking these significant occasions."

Stephen Sapp, Ph.D.
University of Miami
Editor, *Journal of Religious Gerontology*

"One of Sandra DeGidio's great gifts is her ability to help us pray from the experiences of our lives, those experiences we have in common with others and those that are personal and unique. Sandy, like the Psalmist, gives prayerful expression to our joys, our longings, our fears, our laments, but she does this using images and language from the contemporary culture.

"This book is a sensitive work, containing prayer services that will tap into the lives of thousands of elderly individuals to help them understand and express their personal and communal histories as part of their journey to God."

Jane E. Poe
Vice President, Mission Services
Catholic Health Corporation

GIVING COMFORT AND JOY

Prayer Services for the Elderly

Sandra DeGidio, OSM

TWENTY-THIRD PUBLICATIONS
Mystic, Connecticut 06355

Acknowledgment

The English translation of Psalms 42, 57, 63, 66, 103, 139, and 141 from the *Liturgical Psalter* © 1994, International Committee on English in the Liturgy, Inc. All rights reserved.

Second printing 1996

Twenty-Third Publications
185 Willow Street
P.O. Box 180
Mystic, CT 06355
(203) 536-2611
800-321-0411

ISBN 0-89622-685-9
Library of Congress Catalog Card Number 95-61900
Printed in the U.S.A.

Dedication

To Linda Piotrowski
who conceived the idea of this book,
encouraged me to write it
and assisted in its development

Contents

Introduction   1

Liturgical Seasons

An Advent Ritual   10

Festival of Lights (Hanukkah)   12

Blessing of Christmas Tree and Creche   14

An Epiphany Prayer   15

Psalm Prayers for the Weeks of Lent   16

    First Week of Lent   16

    Second Week of Lent   19

    Third Week of Lent   22

    Fourth Week of Lent   26

    Fifth Week of Lent   30

Come, Spirit, Come   34

Minor Church Feasts

New Year's Day   40

Feast of St. Blaise (February 3)   45

St. Valentine's Day   47

Mardi Gras   49

Blessing of St. Joseph's Table   51

Feasts of Mary   52

Feast of Angels (September 29)   55

St. Nicholas Day (December 6)   57

Celebratory Days and Special Occasions

A Birthday or Anniversary Ritual   60

Civic Holidays   62

Celebrating Caregivers   64

Celebrating the Seasons   69

    Spring   71

    Summer   73

    Autumn   74

    Winter   75

Communal Reconciliation Service   76

Memorial Service   80

Memorial Rosary   84

Welcoming a New Resident   86

Blessing for a Sick Resident   88

When Someone Is Hospitalized   90

Thanksgiving for Improved Health or Return from Hospital   91

When a Resident Dies   94

In Times of Sadness, Anxiety, Frustration, Doubt   96

When Concerned for Family or Friends   99

On the Death of an Adult Child   100

In Thanksgiving for Good News   103

Introduction

Linda, a chaplain in a large Extended Care Facility, delights in telling the story of the spontaneous liturgical dance that concluded a prayer service she conducted for a group of residents in the early stages of Alzheimer's disease:

The music therapist and I invited and escorted the folks to our place of prayer. Once everyone was gathered, we had our usual greeting and introductions to remind the residents who we were. I prayed a brief opening prayer, we sang a familiar hymn, and proclaimed a short Scripture passage. We talked a bit about the Scripture reading, and sang an Alleluia.

Then I invited the residents to pray for a son, daughter, wife, husband, friend. I helped them with this by mentioning specific names to jog their memories. For those who could not remember or articulate what they wanted, I stood beside them and prayed for someone I knew was important to them. Edna, who is no longer able to speak, cried silently, yet she smiled when I prayed for her granddaughter Lisa, who visits her regularly.

After all had offered personal prayers, we together prayed the Lord's Prayer. Blanche, who speaks in a repetitive pattern, uttering the same few phrases endlessly, prayed the entire prayer aloud with us, then returned to her recital of two or three phrases.

To close the service, I asked the group for suggestions for a closing song—knowing that responses could range anywhere from "Amazing Grace" to "The Beer Barrel Polka." Nevertheless, we always sing what is suggested. It is, after all, their prayer, not mine.

Fred, who resides at the facility along with his wife, Florence, asked to sing "Let Me Call You Sweetheart." As we began to sing, he painfully got up from his chair, reached out his hand to Florence, and they slowly and cautiously began to dance.

We know that dance releases the inner spirit. For many residents of Extended Care and Group Homes, the body is too weak or weary to actually dance. Still, prayer and ritual experiences for residents in these homes can be poignant and profound more often than one might think.

Spiritual well-being is crucial to successful aging. When all else goes, spirituality remains, a strength that can endure to the end. Continued spiritual development for many older adults in Extended Care and Group Homes is directly related to their participation in worship and prayer experiences. Prayer and rituals help them respond to their inner needs and express their faith. Ritual is an integral part of life; human beings, regardless of their age, are natural ritualizers. Through ritual—the combination of story, symbol, and action—we are all enabled to express the faith that is often difficult to verbalize.

Sacraments, liturgical celebrations, rituals, prayers, readings, hymns can all be expressions of spiritual, social, and psychological well-being. If people are deprived of customary rituals, they may become anxious or depressed. Engaging in the familiar can be a source of strength and hope for them.

Prayer and ritual experiences can also become an arena for the expression of feelings and emotions. Few other opportunities allow silent or verbal expressions of sadness and joy, grief and peace, loss and contentment.

Extended Care and Group Homes are, by their very nature, communities. We need to continue to find ways for these specialized communities to pray together. The spiritual community helps the elderly find inner strength. Looking inward is one aspect of the spiritual life at any age. Looking outward, giving back to the community—and thereby staying connected to the larger world—is the other. Communal prayer in Extended Care facilities can become a shared sacrament through which residents are enabled to care for others while being cared for.

Facilitating participation in prayer and rituals in Extended Care and Group Home settings calls for specialized and creative methods of involvement. As a liturgist, I am keenly aware that creative and meaningful prayer experiences such as Linda's take time to prepare. I am also aware that pastoral ministers who work in these settings often do not have the time to devote to the development of such prayer experiences. At the same time, I have observed how prayer and ritual in these settings can be a source of comfort, joy, and peace for the residents who participate in them.

It is out of these awarenesses and observations, and the prompting of chaplain and pastoral care friends involved in Extended Care, that *Prayer Services for the Elderly* was conceived.

This book is a resource for anyone who is called upon to prepare and lead prayer services for residents of Extended Care and Group Homes. It is designed to be a prayer and ritual aid for chaplains and pastoral care ministers like Linda, as well as for clergy and parish pastoral care ministers who visit these Homes on a regular basis.

Prayer Services for the Elderly is also offered as a gift to residents of Extended Care and Group Homes. The care they receive in these facilities is as much a matter of the spiritual as of the physical.

It is my hope that these prayer services will enhance their continued religious and spiritual development, help their mundane moments become sacred, and make their memories sacramental.

Prayer and Ritual with Third Agers

The story is told that when John Quincy Adams was approaching his eightieth year, he was hobbling down the street one day in his favorite city of Boston, leaning heavily on a cane. A friend approached, slapped him on the shoulder and said, "How's John Quincy this morning?"

Adams turned slowly, smiled, and said:

Fine, Sir, fine. But this old tenement that John Quincy lives in is not so good. The underpinning is about to fall away. The thatch is all gone off the roof. The windows are so dim that John Quincy can hardly see out any more. As a matter of fact, it wouldn't surprise me if before the winter's over, he had to move out altogether. But as for John Quincy Adams, he never was better. Never better.

The physical, psychological, social, and reli-

gious changes that come with aging create challenges for the elderly. And not all the elderly respond to those challenges as sanguinely as John Q. Adams. These challenges necessitate a need for adaptation in prayer and worship with Third Agers, an apt description of the elderly.

Creative approaches to prayer and ritual require a sensitivity to these changing and challenging needs of older adults. Such awareness on the part of prayer leaders will help enhance the spiritual well-being of the elderly and set an example for the rest of the praying community. Then, in any situation, participants will be able to celebrate their spirituality.

In any setting, the elderly can participate in an ongoing sense of prayer, worship, and continued growth in personal spirituality, provided appropriate accommodations are made to respond to these challenges.

Challenges to Self

The Third Age, especially for those confined to Extended Care and Group Homes, brings with it experiences of loss and diminishment that deeply affect self-esteem. The losses may seem to be mainly external, but they are internalized and can decrease self-worth. Relinquishment of home, deaths of spouses and friends, declining health and strength frequently shatter a sense of value or usefulness. Their need for additional assistance with daily activities such as dressing, bathing, medication monitoring, etc., triggers a loss of autonomy.

Inviting residents to choose or suggest songs, to pray prayers of petition and thanksgiving, to comment on a Scripture reading can enhance their self-esteem and self-determination. Asking them to contribute to the prayer can be empowering. More cognitive residents might even be invited to proclaim a Scripture reading or Psalm.

Challenges of Loneliness

Despite planned social activities provided in Extended Care and Group Homes, the elderly who are confined to a room or small apartment can experience a sense of loneliness and isolation. There is a theory that such isolation fosters private devotion and that elders become increasingly more pious. For some that may be true. Others, however, may become bitter. Participation in communal prayer and ritual can help alleviate a sense of bitterness or loneliness.

Some residents respond well to large gatherings; others are more responsive to smaller groups. It is important to provide both approaches. Some residents will be too frail for either. They may be bed-bound or in need of one-to-one ministry. The *Rite of Anointing and Pastoral Care of the Sick* has numerous options for use with these people. In some cases, depending on the frailty of the person, some of the more mobile residents may be able to join in a prayer or ritual in the room of the bed-bound person. This can foster needed socialization and

a sense of community for the person who may feel very much alone.

Residents who attend worship or prayer services not of their past religious background often respond to the inclusiveness of a non-denominational faith experience. In such situations, feelings of isolation can give way to a sense of connectedness.

Challenges to Hearing

As people grow older, auditory acuity may decrease. Hearing loss in older persons can result in a feeling of being shut out from the world around them. If residents are not able to hear during prayer, they may be reluctant to participate in religious services. A totally verbal prayer which they may be unable to hear clearly will have little meaning to them. They may get restless and even become disruptive.

Respond to the hearing-impaired by seating them closest to the prayer leader. Use symbols and ritual to compensate for what they may not be able to hear clearly. Be sure that hearing devices are on and have active batteries. Know which is the good ear, arrange seating accordingly, and speak into that ear. Stand where the person can see you clearly and read your lips if necessary. Speak slowly and distinctly. If the room is large, such as a chapel, use an adequate public address system. Harsh sounds, including brass musical instruments can be distressing to those with hearing aids and should be avoided.

Challenges of Sight

As with hearing loss, diminished eyesight can also cause a feeling of being shut out. If they are unable to see what is going on during prayer, they may be reluctant to participate. They may also respond by becoming restless and disruptive.

Adequate lighting is essential for those with failing eyesight. See that glasses are on and clean. Watch for shadows or glare that may obstruct you or ritual actions. Make certain that sight-impaired persons are seated closest to any ritual action that may be part of the prayer. Use large print for worship aids, music, or prayer copies.

Challenges to Mobility

Canes, crutches, walkers, and wheelchairs restrict the pace of the elderly. Long walks can be fatiguing and discourage participation in prayer. Those with impaired memory and short attention spans may forget where they are going and never arrive.

The place of prayer should be as close as possible to the participants' rooms. Help escort residents to the place of prayer. Make the journey a pleasant one. Engage in small talk, sing a song. Help orient the more cognitively impaired to reality by reminding them that they are on the way to prayer. Ask what they might want to pray for.

Prayer services are best conducted in such a way that people can remain seated throughout, since some will be unable to stand or kneel. During eucharistic liturgies, those unable to stand should be made to feel comfortable remaining seated while others are standing or kneeling. See that they are seated in areas where their view is not obstructed.

While many of the residents may not be able to move about easily, they may be able to clap to music or tap their feet. Feel free to include such action in the prayer and ritual. Such activity can also enhance their physical well-being.

Challenges of Cognition

Residents with memory loss, Alzheimer's disease, and related dementia often respond well to familiar symbols, rituals, hymns, and prayers that connect them with the past. Often persons with severe memory loss are able to recall familiar hymns, prayers, scripture passages, and rites. For these residents, as well as those less memory-impaired, celebrating holy days and minor feasts such as St. Blaise and the blessing of throats helps keep alive their sense of religious tradition.

Short prayer and rituals are best. Be sure that they are lively enough to hold attention, yet calming enough to invite participation. Beginning the services with the Sign of the Cross will often be an instant reminder to those with memory loss that they are about to pray. Hymns with simple refrains are most practical. Repetition is very effective in praying with the cognitively impaired. Short, repeated, sung or spoken responses often elicit enthusiastic response.

Challenges of Skin Hunger

Kinetic experiences are important to all of us. Some of the best nurses and nursing assistants in Extended Care and Group Homes are those who incorporate high touch techniques. They rub sore backs; they hug residents at appropriate times; they kiss foreheads and bless residents as they tuck them in at night. Incorporating touch and symbols of touch in prayer is extremely helpful in prayer with the elderly. Using lotions, oils, hand massage, signs of peace, hand-holding, and gestures of blessing can help alleviate many fears, and meet needs experienced by older adults. Non-verbal communication comes through even when cognitive ability is gone.

Challenges to Third Age Spirituality

Creative approaches to prayer and ritual that focus on old learning and familiar experiences are particularly effective with the elderly. Familiar religious symbols—rosaries, candles, prayer books, a cross, statues, icons, liturgical colors, and clergy vestments—encourage responses and provide a focus for diminishing attention spans. Symbols and visual props such as pictures, flowers, prayer books, a cross or rosary, when held by participants, can evoke a quieting or centering response.

In many ways, prayer and ritual with the aging is a ministry of memory. One of the ways of addressing such a ministry is to keep a Memory Book which lists the names of those in the facility who have died. Periodically conduct a prayer service for those people. Invite family members to join residents and staff for these services.

Storytelling is another effective technique when praying with older adults. We never outgrow our enjoyment of stories. For the elderly, it is a particularly productive method of unlocking memories of past rituals and celebrations. Through story, persons with Alzheimer's disease and other forms of memory loss can continue to respond to their faith and inner needs.

Even though someone is cognitively impaired, the ultimate questions are still there. Long-remembered stories and rituals help them connect their past with the present. Prayers and hymns are still familiar, and when repeated several times, the person will often participate.

Because of the physical, psychosocial, and spiritual condition of residents in Extended Care and Group Homes, it is important to make prayer services lively enough to allow spirits to soar and eyes to dance. It is equally important that these services be simple enough to hold interest, and relaxed enough to invite participation.

Simplicity and flexibility are key to praying with the elderly. Simplifying prayers, responses, rituals, ceremonies, homilies, and Scripture commentaries is essential. When organizing and leading prayer for persons with memory loss, flexibility is an indispensable attribute. All plans can change at a moment's notice. Remember, prayer rises from the community.

Sensitivity to these physical, psychosocial, and spiritual challenges of Third Agers is fundamental to the prayer services and rituals that follow.

Using This Book

These prayer services and rituals can be used as presented or adapted to meet your particular needs. You are encouraged to be creative in preparing the prayers and rituals to meet the individual needs of your community. For example, you may wish to have music where none is indicated, or to use a spoken refrain where a sung refrain is suggested. Scripture or story recommendations may not be quite right for your group. Feel free to choose those that best meet your needs. Individual situations may also call for a change in the ritual format. Make these prayer services unique and distinctive for your particular needs.

If copies of the prayer services are needed or appropriate for your group, the pages of this book may be duplicated for that purpose. The following suggestions for adaptation are offered for maximum effectiveness:

Preparation
Always be prepared and be familiar with the service. Even though the services may seem easy to follow, it is important that you are familiar with each one before attempting to lead it.

Remember, flexibility is key. To be flexible, one must be totally comfortable with what is prepared.

Themes
The prayer services and rituals offered are divided into three basic themes: Liturgical Seasons, Minor Church Feasts, Celebratory Days and Special Occasions. Some of the Special Occasions services can be prayed either communally or individually, with some adaptation. It is recommended that you acquaint yourself with all the services in advance, so that you will be able to return to them at appropriate times.

Setting
The elderly can participate in an ongoing sense of communal prayer, worship, and a lifelong growth in personal devotion in almost any setting. It is important to be familiar with the group you are leading. For some services, the chapel serves well. For others, a smaller space with the fewest possible distractions is more advantageous.

Scripture

Readings from Scripture should always be short. Sometimes a poignant sentence or two, such as "God is love and all who live in love live in God and God lives in them," is sufficient. If a Scripture story is used, it may be better told as a story rather than read. In any case, Scripture is best proclaimed with the Bible in hand, even if the story is told. The book of Scriptures will serve as a familiar symbol to residents. A brief period of silence following the proclamation of Scripture is advisable.

Homily/Scripture Commentary

This should be a brief reflection on the reading—two or three minutes at most. In some cases, the commentary can be a group reflection. Asking appropriate questions to elicit reactions from the participants facilitates such dialogue.

Responses

Spoken or sung responses should be short: a few words such as "Hear us, O Lord," "Love one another," "Thank you, God, for giving us life," or a sung "Alleluia." During liturgical seasons such as Advent and Lent, the same response might be used in all prayer services, including Eucharist, throughout the season.

Intercessions

Intercessions, or prayers of petition, can include personal petitions. Those gathered for prayer may be invited and encouraged to pray for someone or something that is important to them. Mentioning a husband, wife, son, or daughter helps. Often, hearing the name of the person evokes a memory and a response. Sometimes the leader may need to name a person or need for which a non-articulate resident may wish to pray.

Passing or carrying a lighted Prayer Candle to the resident offering an intercession can help focus attention on the prayer and provide a bit of personal attention for the resident as well.

Music

In some cases, music suggestions are given in the prayer services and rituals. In other cases, music is suggested but not specified. Feel free to insert music that is appropriate for your group. If you are not comfortable leading the music, recorded music can be helpful. Always be open to music suggestions from the group. Sing what is requested, whatever it may be.

Symbols

Use symbols liberally. They help to hold the residents' attention and often speak more loudly than words. Symbols can be common religious symbols such as water, oil, light, bread, wine, and candles. They can also be ordinary natural symbols such as autumn leaves, flowers, Christmas wreaths or garlands, candy canes. Beginning services with the Sign of the Cross can serve as an automatic call to prayer. In arranging the environment for prayer, keep seasonal liturgical colors in mind. They, too, can evoke memories and cue residents to prayer.

Audiovisuals

Slides and recorded music can enhance prayer with Third Agers. Playing a recording of Taizé chants, Gregorian Chant, instrumental or other sacred music reminiscent of the past, as participants gather, can be calming and soothing. Sometimes a single slide projected during the entire prayer can hold attention. At other times, a series of slides might accompany the praying of a Psalm or the Stations of the Cross. Slides of familiar religious landmarks of the area are also effective.

In developing your prayer services and rituals, keep the particular group with whom you are praying uppermost in your mind. And feel free to use your creativity and sense of celebration.

Following are two general prayer formats that you can use at any time, and particularly during Ordinary Time. Fill in your own Introduction, Prayers, Hymns, Scriptures, ritual actions, etc.

Prayer Format A

Introduction
  Greeting and informal introduction of leader
Sign of the Cross
Opening Prayer
  Brief. Center the prayer on observable things such as the season, the weather, events in the Home, the focus of the prayer, etc.
Hymn
Scripture Reading
  A very short passage, one or two sentences at most
Psalm Response or Alleluia
  Spoken or sung. One line at most, e.g.: "Glory and praise to our God."
Gospel Reading
  Short
Psalm Response or Alleluia
  Repeated from above
Reflection on Scriptures
  An extremely short commentary on the reading given by the leader. Use visuals (flowers, a stuffed animal, books, candles) to help hold attention.
Prayers of Petition
  Invite individuals to pray for someone or something. Use a short response such as "We pray to the Lord." Mention husbands, wives, daughters, sons, grandchildren, etc. If possible, refer to these people by name to help jog memories.
The Lord's Prayer
Gesture of Peace
Closing Hymn
  Have one planned, but invite suggestions.

Prayer Format B

Introduction
  Greeting and informal introduction of leader
Sign of the Cross
Hymn
Opening Prayer
  Brief
Scripture Reading
  A very short passage, one or two sentences at most
Sung Psalm Response or Alleluia
Ritual Action
  Related to the Scripture passage, for example, laying on of hands, anointing with oil, lighting of candles, breaking and sharing of bread
Sung Psalm Response or Alleluia
  Repeated from above
Prayers of Petition
  Invite individuals to pray for someone or something. Use a short response such as "We pray to the Lord." Mention husbands, wives, daughters, sons, grandchildren, etc. If possible, refer to these people by name to help jog memories.
The Lord's Prayer
Closing Hymn
  Have one planned, but invite suggestions.
Gesture of Friendship
  Share an appropriate snack.

Liturgical Seasons

An Advent Ritual

Materials Needed
A 25-foot artificial evergreen garland with intertwined electrical Christmas lights, a Bible

Preparation and Environment
Arrange chairs in a semi-circle near an electrical outlet. Leave space for wheelchairs. Place the garland on the floor in front of the chairs.

Introduction
Greeting and introduction by leader. Remind participants of the season of Advent, a time of movement from darkness to light and the coming of Christ, the Light of the World.

Hymn
"O Come, O Come, Emmanuel"
(Depending on the group, you may want to simply repeat the first line of the hymn.)

Sign of the Cross

Opening Prayer
Leader Come, Lord Jesus. It is winter time. Days are short and nights are long. We need your warmth, your light, your love, and your hope. Come, Lord Jesus; be with us as we pray.

Hymn
"O Come, O Come, Emmanuel" (or first line only repeated 2 or 3 times)
(While the hymn is being sung, move the garland from the floor to the laps and hands of the participants.)

Scripture
Mark 8:22–26 or 10:46–52
(Depending on the group, you may wish to tell the story while holding the Bible.)

Response
"O Come, O Come, Emmanuel" *(sung, first line repeated 2 or 3 times)*

Scripture
Luke 11:33–36 or Matthew 5:14–16

Response

"O Come, O Come, Emmanuel" *(sung, first line repeated 2 or 3 times)*

Reflection on Scripture

Short commentary on darkness and light and how Jesus called us to be light for one another. At the conclusion of the commentary, plug in the garland and enjoy the multi-colored lights that were unnoticed without a source of power and energy. Talk about the importance of being connected to Christ, who is the Light of the World.

Response

"This Little Light of Mine" *(sung)*

Festival of Lights
(Hanukkah)

This ritual can be celebrated once, at the end of Hanukkah, or repeated each day for the eight days of Hanukkah. Celebrating the ritual for all eight days of the Feast would be particularly valuable if there are a number of Jewish people in your facility.

Materials Needed
9-branched candle holder, 9 small candles, one for each day (3 1/2 inch birthday candles work best). The candelabra (called *menorah* in Hebrew) can be made out of spools attached to a base, tinkertoys assembled in a variety of ways, clay, a piece of wood with 9 holes drilled into it, etc.

Background
The feast of Hanukkah lasts eight days. One candle is lit the first day, two the second, etc. The center hole in the menorah is for the "servant candle" that is used to light the others each evening. The reason for the small candles is that, by custom, the lights are allowed to burn out each evening. While this happens, nothing is done except to watch, to pray, and to enjoy the light, the darkness, and the quiet.

As part of the ritual, participants might be invited to exchange small gifts they may have made in activities sessions.

Like Christmas, Hanukkah has its origins in the change that happens to the sun during this season. And, like Christmas, Hanukkah has its historic occasion. In the second century before Christ, the Jewish brothers known as the Maccabees led a victorious revolt against the foreign occupiers of the land and were able to reclaim and rededicate the temple in Jerusalem (the word Hanukkah means "dedication").

The legend says that when the temple was recaptured, all the sacred oil had been profaned except for a one-day supply. It would take eight days to sanctify new oil. But a miracle happened and a tiny bit of holy oil burned for the whole eight days.

Preparation and Environment
Arrange chairs in a semi-circle, leaving space for wheelchairs. Place the menorah on a table where it can be seen by all. Have the room dimly lit.

Introduction
Greeting and introduction of leader.
(Remind participants of the feast of Hanukkah and its background.)

The Service
Light the "servant candle" and recite the blessing:

Leader   Blessed are you, Lord our God.

All   Blessed are you, Lord our God.

Leader   Blessed are you, Lord our God, ruler of the universe.
You have given us life and permitted us to reach this season.

All   Blessed are you, Lord our God.

Leader   Blessed are you, Lord our God, ruler of the universe.
You have sanctified us with your commandments
and commanded us to kindle the lights of Hanukkah.

All   Blessed are you, Lord our God.

Leader   Blessed are you, Lord our God, ruler of the universe.
You performed miracles for our ancestors in those days, at this season.

All   Blessed are you, Lord our God.

Scripture (optional)
(Invite and assist participants to light the candles).

Leader   We kindle these lights on account of the miracles, wonders, and deliverances which you performed for our ancestors. These lights are sacred throughout the eight days of Hanukkah; we are not permitted to make any use of them, but only to look at them, in order to give thanks to you.

Song
"Prepare Ye" from "Godspell" or "O Come, O Come, Emmanuel"
(In silence, let the candles burn out and then remain silent for a few moments in the darkness.)

Gift-Giving
Invite participants to exchange gifts they have made. Although not a usual part of the service, you might wish to add a short Scripture reading each day. The following suggestions introduce a different prophet each day and bring a note of the Advent season into the Hanukkah celebration:

First day: Amos 5:14–15
Second day: Hosea 2:18–20
Third day: Joel 3:1–3
Fourth day: Jeremiah 33:14–16

Fifth day: Isaiah 7:14
Sixth day: Ezekiel 37:1–10
Seventh day: Isaiah 40:3–5
Eighth day: Malachi 3:1

Blessing of Christmas Tree and Creche

In a small procession, participants can carry the creche figures to their place of honor and hang some ornaments on the tree.

Blessing Prayer

Leader God of Love, bless this creche we have prepared
in remembrance of the birth of your Son.
We ask that the light of Christ's goodness
shine on all of us here. Amen.
(Sprinkle the creche with holy water; incense may also be used. Plug in the Christmas lights.)

Leader God of Life and Light,
we ask your blessing upon this tree.
May its ever-greenness
be a sign of the hope of the Christmas season,
its glittering ornaments
a sign of the joy of the Christmas season,
and the gifts beneath it
a sign of the love of the Christmas season.
Amen.
(Sprinkle the tree with holy water.)

Leader For the wonder of birth and life,

All We thank you, God.

Leader For this day to remember the birth of Jesus in Bethlehem,

All We thank you, God.

Leader For the joy and wonder of this Christmas season,

All We thank you, God.

Leader For the love we share at this time of year,

All We thank you, God.

Leader Let us sing with the angels, with the cattle and the sheep, with the shepherds and the stars of heaven, with Joseph and Mary *(sing a Christmas carol)*.

Gesture of Friendship
Share tea and Christmas cookies.

An Epiphany Prayer

Materials Needed
Christmas creche, figures of the Magi, candle, bundt cake(s) decorated to resemble a crown.

Preparation and Environment
Gather participants around the Christmas creche. In a short procession, bring in the figures representing the Magi and place them among the other creche figures.

Introduction
Leader   Today we celebrate the Feast of Epiphany, the day we commemorate the manifestation of Jesus to the gentiles and the whole world.
(The candle is lighted.)

Leader   Christ is the Light of the World.

All   Christ is the Light of the World.

Opening Song
"We Three Kings"
(During the song, the figures of the Magi are carried to the creche.)

Scripture
Matthew 2:1–12

Shared Prayer
Leader   The Magi brought Jesus gifts of gold, frankincense (incense) and myrrh (scented oil). If you were visiting Jesus today, what would you bring him? *(Individual prayers might begin with "If I were visiting Jesus today, I would bring him the gift of...")*

Concluding Prayer
Gathering our gifts together, let us wrap them in the prayer Jesus taught us. Our Father...

Closing Song

Gesture of Friendship
Share the "crown cake" and coffee or tea.

Psalm Prayers for the Weeks of Lent

These prayers, based on an abbreviated format of the Prayer of the Church, are designed to be used once a week during the season of Lent. Depending on the group, you may need to abbreviate them even further.

Note: Use incense sticks that are as lightly scented as possible and be sure that the incense will not be hazardous to those with respiratory problems.

First Week of Lent

Proclamation of Light

(A candle and an incense stick are lit.)

Leader   Rejoice, O people of God!
Christ, the Light, is present among us.
May our prayer rise like incense before you.
Let us live in the Light.

All   Let us live in the Light.

Thanksgiving for the Light

Leader   Merciful God,
in these forty days you lead us on a pilgrimage of repentance,
that through prayer and penance,
we might learn once more to be your faithful people.
Let us live in the Light.

All   Let us live in the Light.

Leader   Light our hearts with the fire of your love.
Open our eyes to the tenderness of your care.
Free us to forgive and accept forgiveness.
Let us live in the Light.

All   Let us live in the Light.

Leader   Be with us in these days
that we may overcome whatever blinds us.
Set us free
to live in the glorious light of your Son Jesus Christ,
who lives and reigns with you in the Holy Spirit,
one God, forever and ever.

All   Amen.

Psalmody
Psalm 141:1–4, 8–10

Antiphon
Grant to us, O Lord, a heart renewed. *(sung)*

Reader   Hurry, Lord! I call and call!
Listen! I plead with you.
Let my prayer rise like incense,
my upraised hands,
like an evening sacrifice.

All   Grant to us, O Lord, a heart renewed.

Reader   Lord, guard my lips,
watch my every word.
Let me never speak evil
or consider hateful deeds,
let me never join the wicked
to eat their lavish meals.

All   Grant to us, O Lord, a heart renewed.

Reader   Lord my God, I turn to you,
in you I find safety.
Do not strip me of life.
Do not spring on me
the traps of the wicked.
Let evildoers get tangled
in their own nets,
but let me escape.

All   Grant to us, O Lord, a heart renewed.

Psalm Prayer
Leader   Merciful God,
in faith and love we call upon you.
Hear our prayer during this lenten season
and watch over us now and always.

All   Amen.

Intercessions

Leader   Merciful God, we know you hear our prayer, and so we pray:

Reader   We lift our hands in thanksgiving...
              Lord, have mercy.

All   Lord, have mercy.

Reader   We renew our efforts to do good...
              Lord, have mercy.

All   Lord, have mercy.

Reader   We stand firm against evil...
              Lord, have mercy.

All   Lord, have mercy.

Reader   We pray for the sick...
              Lord, have mercy.

All   Lord, have mercy.

Reader   We pray for the dead...
              Lord, have mercy.

All   Lord, have mercy.

Our Father...

Concluding Prayer

Leader   O God, you renew us by our celebration of Lent.
              Grant us fresh strength to meet the challenges of this week,
                  that we may come to you faithfully now and always.

All   Amen.

Blessing

Leader   May Almighty God protect and bless us in the name of the Father, and of the Son, and of the Holy Spirit. Amen.

Second Week of Lent

Proclamation of Light

(A candle and an incense stick are lit.)

Leader Rejoice, O people of God;
    Christ, the Light, is present among us.
Let us live in the Light.

All Let us live in the Light.

Thanksgiving for the Light

Leader Merciful God, in these forty days you lead us on a pilgrimage of repentance, that through prayer and penance, we might learn once more to be your faithful people. Let us live in the Light.

All Let us live in the Light.

Leader Light our hearts with the fire of your love. Open our eyes to the tenderness of your care. Free us to forgive and accept forgiveness. Let us live in the Light.

All Let us live in the Light.

Leader Be with us in these days that we may overcome whatever blinds us. Set us free to live in the glorious light of your Son Jesus Christ, who lives and reigns with you in the Holy Spirit, one God, forever and ever.

All Amen.

Psalmody
Psalm 63:1–9

Antiphon
Grant to us, O Lord, a heart renewed. *(sung)*

Reader God, my God, you I crave;
my soul thirsts for you,
my body aches for you
like a dry and weary land.
Let me gaze on you in your temple:
a vision of strength and glory.

All Grant to us, O Lord, a heart renewed.

Reader Your love is better than life,
my speech is full of praise.
I give you a lifetime of worship,
my hands raised in your name.
I feast at a rich table,
my lips sing of your glory.

All Grant to us, O Lord, a heart renewed.

Reader On my bed I lie awake,
your memory fills the night.
You have been my help,
I rejoice beneath your wings.
Yes, I cling to you,
your right hands holds me fast.

All Grant to us, O Lord, a heart renewed.

Psalm Prayer
Leader O God whom we seek,
your love is better than life.
Keep us in the shadow of your wings
as we celebrate this season of Lent.

All Amen.

Intercessions
Leader Merciful God, we know you hear our prayer, and so we pray:

Reader We recognize our frailty...
Lord, have mercy.

All Lord, have mercy.

Reader We renew our efforts to do good...
Lord, have mercy.

All Lord, have mercy.

Reader We refuse to sin with our tongues...
Lord, have mercy.

All Lord, have mercy.

Reader We pray for the sick...
Lord, have mercy.

All Lord, have mercy.

Reader We pray for the dead...
Lord, have mercy.

All Lord, have mercy.

Our Father...

Concluding Prayer

Leader O God, you renew us by our celebration of Lent.
Grant us fresh strength to meet the challenges of this week,
that we may come to you faithfully now and always.

All Amen.

Blessing

Leader May Almighty God protect and bless us in the name of the Father, and of the Son, and of the Holy Spirit.

All Amen.

Third Week of Lent

Proclamation of Light

(A candle and an incense stick are lit.)

Leader   Rejoice, O people of God;
  Christ, the Light, is present among us.
  Let us live in the Light.

All   Let us live in the Light.

Thanksgiving for the Light

Leader   Merciful God, in these forty days you lead us on a pilgrimage of repentance, that through prayer and penance we might learn once more to be your faithful people. Let us live in the Light.

All   Let us live in the Light.

Leader   Light our hearts with the fire of your love. Open our eyes to the tenderness of your care and free us to forgive and accept forgiveness. Let us live in the Light.

All   Let us live in the Light.

Leader   Be with us in these days that we may overcome whatever blinds us. Set us free to live in the glorious light of your Son Jesus Christ, who lives and reigns with you in the Holy Spirit, one God, forever and ever.

All   Amen.

Psalmody
Psalm 66:1–12, 19–20

Antiphon
Grant to us, O Lord, a heart renewed. *(sung)*

Reader   All earth, shout with joy to God!
  Sing the glory of the Name!
  Give glorious praise!
  Say, "How awesome your works!"

All   Grant to us, O Lord, a heart renewed.

Reader Because of your mighty strength,
your enemies cringe before you.
All earth bows before you,
sings to you, sings to your name.

All Grant to us, O Lord, a heart renewed.

Reader Come, see God's wonders,
tremendous deeds for the people:
God turned sea into land,
they crossed the river on foot.

All Grant to us, O Lord, a heart renewed.

Reader Let us rejoice then in God,
who rules for ever with might,
keeping watch on all nations.
Let no rebels raise their heads!

All Grant to us, O Lord, a heart renewed.

Reader Bless our God, you peoples,
loudly sound God's praise,
who kept our spirits alive
and our feet from stumbling.

All Grant to us, O Lord, a heart renewed.

Reader God, you have tested us,
refined us like silver in fire.
You led us into a trap,
you put a weight on our backs,
you let others beat us down.
We passed through water and fire,
but then you brought us relief.

All Grant to us, O Lord, a heart renewed.

Reader Bless God who did listen,
heeded the sound of my prayer.
God did not reject my plea,
but pledged me constant love.

All   Grant to us, O Lord, a heart renewed.

Psalm Prayer
Leader   Merciful God,
  your works are mighty and great.
As you led your people of old
  from slavery to freedom,
  so lead us during this lenten season.

All   Amen.

Intercessions
Leader   Merciful God, we know you hear our prayer, and so we pray:

Reader   To recognize God's awesome deeds...
Lord, have mercy.

All   Lord, have mercy.

Reader   To surrender ourselves to God's power...
Lord, have mercy.

All   Lord, have mercy.

Reader   To follow God's call...
Lord, have mercy.

All   Lord, have mercy.

Reader   We pray for the sick...
Lord, have mercy.

All   Lord, have mercy.

Reader   We pray for the dead...
Lord, have mercy.

All   Lord, have mercy.

Our Father...

Concluding Prayer

Leader   O God, you renew us by our celebration of Lent.
Grant us fresh strength to meet the challenges of this week,
      that we may come to you faithfully now and always.

All   Amen.

Blessing

Leader   May Almighty God protect and bless us in the name of the Father, and of the Son, and of the Holy Spirit. Amen.

Fourth Week of Lent

Proclamation of Light

(A candle and an incense stick are lit.)

Leader Rejoice, O people of God;
Christ, the Light is present among us.
Let us live in the Light.

All Let us live in the Light.

Thanksgiving for the Light

Leader Merciful God, in these forty days you lead us on a pilgrimage of repentance, that through prayer and penance, we might learn once more to be your faithful people. Let us live in the Light.

All Let us live in the Light.

Leader Light our hearts with the fire of your love. Open our eyes to the tenderness of your care. Free us to forgive and accept forgiveness. Let us live in the Light.

All Let us live in the Light.

Leader Be with us in these days that we may overcome whatever blinds us. Set us free to live in the glorious light of your Son Jesus Christ, who lives and reigns with you in the Holy Spirit, one God, forever and ever.

All Amen.

Psalmody
Psalm 42

Antiphon
Grant to us, O Lord, a heart renewed. *(sung)*

Reader As a deer craves running water,
I thirst for you, my God;
I thirst for God,
the living God.
When will I see your face?

All Grant to us, O Lord, a heart renewed.

Reader Tears are my steady diet,
Day and night I hear,
"Where is your God?"

I cry my heart out,
I remember better days:
when I entered the house of God,
I was caught in the joyful sound
of pilgrims giving thanks.

All Grant to us, O Lord, a heart renewed.

Reader Why are you sad, my heart?
Why do you grieve?
Wait for the Lord.
I will yet praise God my savior.

All Grant to us, O Lord, a heart renewed.

Reader My heart is sad.
Even from Jordan and Hermon,
from the peak of Mizar,
I remember you.

All Grant to us, O Lord, a heart renewed.

Reader There the deep roars to deep;
your torrents crash over me.
The love God summoned by day
sustained my praise by night,
my prayer to the living God.

All Grant to us, O Lord, a heart renewed.

Reader I complain to God
who I thought was rock:
"Why have you forgotten me?
Why am I bent double
under the weight of enemies?

Their insults grind me to dust.
Day and night they say,
'Where is your God?'"

All Grant to us, O Lord, a heart renewed.

Reader Why are you sad, my heart?
Why do you grieve?
Wait for the Lord.
I will yet praise God my savior.

All Grant to us, O Lord, a heart renewed.

Psalm Prayer
Leader Merciful God,
you favor us with your mighty deeds.
May our lenten promises, praise and thanks
be pleasing to you
now and always.

All Amen.

Intercessions
Leader Merciful God, we know you hear our prayer, and so we pray:

Reader We lift our hands in thanksgiving...
Lord, have mercy.

All Lord, have mercy.

Reader We renew our efforts to do good...
Lord, have mercy.

All Lord, have mercy.

Reader We stand firm against evil...
Lord, have mercy.

All Lord, have mercy.

Reader We pray for the sick...
Lord, have mercy.

All Lord, have mercy.

Reader We pray for the dead...
Lord, have mercy.

All   Lord, have mercy.

Our Father...

Concluding Prayer

Leader   O God, you renew us by our celebration of Lent.
Grant us fresh strength to meet the challenges of this week,
   that we may come to you faithfully now and always.

All   Amen.

Blessing

Leader   May Almighty God protect and bless us in the name of the Father, and of the Son.
and of the Holy Spirit.

All   Amen.

Fifth Week of Lent

Proclamation of Light

(A candle and an incense stick are lit.)

Leader   Rejoice, O people of God; Christ, the Light is present among us.
Let us live in the Light.

All   Let us live in the Light.

Thanksgiving for the Light

Leader   Merciful God, in these forty days you lead us on a pilgrimage of repentance, that through prayer and penance, we might learn once more to be your faithful people. Let us live in the Light.

All   Let us live in the Light.

Leader   Light our hearts with the fire of your love. Open our eyes to the tenderness of your care. Free us to forgive and accept forgiveness. Let us live in the Light.

All   Let us live in the Light.

Leader   Be with us in these days that we may overcome whatever blinds us. Set us free to live in the glorious light of your Son Jesus Christ, who lives and reigns with you in the Holy Spirit, one God, forever and ever.

All   Amen.

Psalmody
Psalm 57

Antiphon
Grant to us, O Lord, a heart renewed. *(sung)*

Reader   Care for me, God, take care of me,
I have nowhere else to hide.
Shadow me with your wings
until all danger passes.

All   Grant to us, O Lord, a heart renewed.

Reader   I call to the Most High,
to God, my avenger:

send help from heaven to free me,
punish those who hound me.

All   Grant to us, O Lord, a heart renewed.

Reader   Extend to me, O God,
your love that never fails,
for I find myself among lions
who crave for human flesh,
their teeth like spears and arrows,
their tongues sharp as swords.

All   Grant to us, O Lord, a heart renewed.

Reader   O God, rise high above the heavens!
Spread your glory across the earth!

They rigged a net for me,
a trap to bring me down;
they dug a pit for me,
but they—they fell in!

All   Grant to us, O Lord, a heart renewed.

Reader   I have decided, O God,
my decision is firm:
to you I will sing my praise.
Awake, my soul, to song!

All   Grant to us, O Lord, a heart renewed.

Reader   Awake, my harp and lyre,
so I can wake up the dawn!
I will lift my voice in praise,
sing of you, Lord, to all nations.
For your love reaches heaven's edge,
your unfailing love, the skies.

O God, rise high about the heavens!
Spread your glory across the earth!

All   Grant to us, O Lord, a heart renewed.

Psalm Prayer

Leader Merciful God,
    you created all that is good,
    and watch over all who hear your voice.
    As you led your people from bondage
        to a land of milk and honey,
        so be with us on our lenten journey,
        and lead us to great joy.

All Amen.

Intercessions

Leader Merciful God, we know you hear our prayer, and so we pray:

Reader We recognize our frailty...
    Lord, have mercy.

All Lord, have mercy.

Reader We renew our efforts to do good...
    Lord, have mercy.

All Lord, have mercy.

Reader We refuse to sin with our tongues...
    Lord, have mercy.

All Lord, have mercy.

Reader We pray for the sick...
    Lord, have mercy.

All Lord, have mercy.

Reader We pray for the dead...
    Lord, have mercy.

All Lord, have mercy.

Our Father...

Concluding Prayer

Leader O God, you renew us by our celebration of Lent.
Grant us fresh strength to meet the challenges of this week,
    that we may come to you faithfully now and always.

All Amen.

Blessing

Leader May Almighty God protect and bless us in the name of the Father, and of the Son,
and of the Holy Spirit.

All Amen.

Come, Spirit, Come

This service can be used on the Vigil of Pentecost, the Feast of Pentecost, during Pentecost week, or any time invocation of the Spirit is called for.

Materials Needed
Candle, small fan, wind-chimes, bright-colored lightweight fabric banners

Preparation and Environment
Arrange banners and wind-chimes in such a way that they are moved by the wind of the fan.

Opening Song
"Come, Holy Ghost"

Opening Prayer

Leader Come, Holy Spirit,
    great infuser
    breather of knowledge,
    windy storyteller,
Whistle your wondrous wisdom
    to those who call others to growth.
Yes,
    come, Holy Spirit, and answer this prayer.
We wrap it in the name of Jesus,
    the one we call teacher,
    the one we call Savior,
    the one we name Lord.

Invoking the Spirit
Response: "Lord, send out your Spirit and renew the face of the earth" *(sung)*

All Come, Spirit,

Leader Be with us as light in our darkness.

All Come, Spirit,

Leader Be with us as hope in oppression.

All Come, Spirit,

Leader   Be with us as rain in a drought.

All   Come, Spirit,

Leader   Be with us as life-giving food.

All   Come, Spirit,

Leader   Be with us as warmth in winter.

All   Come, Spirit,

Leader   Be with us through the worst.

Response: "Lord, send out your Spirit and renew the face of the earth."

All   Come, Spirit,

Leader   Visit the unenlightened.

All   Come, Spirit,

Leader   Establish ways of justice.

All   Come, Spirit,

Leader   Banish discrimination.

All   Come, Spirit,

Leader   Break the bread of freedom;
                wash earth's wounds away.

All   Come, Spirit,

Leader   Declare a holy day.

Response: "Lord, send out your Spirit and renew the face of the earth."

All   Come, Spirit,

Leader   As healing and wholeness.

All Come, Spirit,

Leader As peace and perseverance.

All Come, Spirit,

Leader As mercy and grace.

All Come, Spirit,

Leader As forgiveness and blessing.

All Come, Spirit,

Leader As compassion and comfort.
    as all that is good

   Response: "Lord, send out your Spirit and renew the face of the earth."

Leader Come, Spirit, renew our hearts
    as we gather for prayer and praise.
   Renew the earth, now and every day.

   Scripture
   Acts 2:1–4

   Sung Response
   Alleluia

   Litany of the Spirit

All Come!

Leader Breath of God,

All Come!

Leader Star of Morning,

All Come!

Leader Cool of Evening,

All   Come!

Leader   Everlasting hope,

All   Come!

Leader   Love that never ends,

All   Come!

Leader   Source of Illumination,

All   Come!

Leader   Tongues of fire and flame,

All   Come!

Leader   Finger of God's right hand,

All   Come!

Leader   Love that never ends,

All   Come!

Leader   Sign of healing and wholeness,

All   Come!

Leader   Life of the Living God,

All   Come!

Leader   Wisdom and understanding,

All   Come!

Leader   Knowledge and fortitude,

All   Come!

Leader   Caregiver, Comforter,

All   Come!

Leader   Protector of the poor,

All   Come!

Leader   Friend of the utterly alone,

All   Come!

Leader   Gift of all that gives,

All   Come!

Leader   Come, Holy Spirit, come.

Closing Prayer

Leader   Come, Spirit,
       be with us always.
May we live forever in the name of love.
May we love forever in the name of life.
Called by God, filled with the Spirit,
       may we live in the love of the Spirit forever.

All   Amen.

Closing Song
"Come, Holy Ghost" (or other appropriate song)

Minor Church Feasts

New Year's Day

Materials Needed
A Bible, 13 candles, a previous year's calendar, a new calendar (if possible, one for each participant), a basket.

Preparation and Environment
Place 13 candles, Bible, calendars, and a basket on a table that is easily accessible to participants.

Call to Prayer
Leader Let us remember that we are in the holy presence of God. *(The candles are lit.)* We celebrate today a new beginning in the Light of the Lord. A new beginning as the rising sun is the beginning of a new day. Today we celebrate the beginning of a new year and a new beginning for each of us. A new beginning filled with promise and hope, surrounded by the love and the light of Christ.

Opening Song
"Auld Lang Syne"

Opening Prayer
Leader Blessed are you, Lord God of all creation. You have given us life and permitted us to reach this new year. You bless us with many good things and hold out for us the promise of more to come. We thank you for what has been and ask you to guide and protect us in what will be, through Christ our Lord.

All Amen.

Scripture Reading
Ecclesiastes 3:1

Reader To everything there is a season,
and a time to every purpose under heaven.

Thanksgiving Prayer for the Past Year
Using last year's calendar, go through each month, recalling its special moments. Add your own facility's celebrations, admissions, deaths, etc. Invite participants to share remembrances of the month. As each month is remembered, invite a participant to tear the page off the calendar, drop it in the basket and put out a candle.

Leader For all that has been,

All Thank you, Lord.

Leader For the newness that was last January.
For the hope it held and the freshness it gave us.
For the lengthening days revealing the light of Christ to us.
(Personal remembrances)
For all that was of January 19__.

All Thank you, Lord.

Leader For the love that we shared in February; the hearts, the valentines.
For the presidents we remembered and the happiness we shared.
(Personal remembrances)
For all that was of February 19__.

All Thank you, Lord.

Leader For the call to penitence that was Lent.
For St. Patrick and St. Joseph, whom we remembered this month.
(Personal remembrances)
For all that was of March 19__.

All Thank you, Lord.

Leader For springtime and Easter.
For tulips and daffodils.
For crucifixion and resurrection.
(Personal remembrances)
For the New Life that was April 19__.

All Thank you, Lord.

Leader For May poles and May baskets, May flowers and maybes.
For Mary and mothers honored this month.
For those who died defending the rights of others.
(Personal remembrances)
For all that was of May 19__.

All Thank you, Lord.

Leader For bright sun and long days.

For the Pentecost Spirit and the birth of the church.
For fathers honored this month.
(Personal remembrances)
For all that was June 19__.

All   Thank you, Lord.

Leader   For summer days and starlit nights.
For our independence as a country.
For fireworks and freedom.
(Personal remembrances)
For all that was July 19__.

All   Thank you, Lord.

Leader   For families and children enjoying the last fling of summer.
For the fresh fruits of gardens and orchards.
(Personal remembrances)
For all that was of August 19__.

All   Thank you, Lord.

Leader   For the beginning of autumn and a new school year for children.
For angels remembered this month and full harvest moons.
(Personal remembrances)
For all that was of September 19__.

All   Thank you, Lord.

Leader   For multi-colored leaves and change.
For Mary and the prayer we call the rosary.
For St. Francis and St. Teresa, whom we remembered this month.
(Personal remembrances)
For all that was of October 19__.

All   Thank you, Lord.

Leader   For the saints of the church.
For the saints of our families, whom we remembered this month.
For a special day to give thanks.
(Personal remembrances)
For all that was of November 19__.

All   Thank you, Lord.

Leader   For Advent and waiting.
             For Christmas and births.
             For endings of years.
             (Personal remembrances)
             For all that was of December 19__.

All   Thank you, Lord.

Scripture Reading
Ecclesiastes 3:1

Reader   To everything there is a season,
             and a time to every purpose under heaven.

Blessing of New Calendars
Leader   *(Hold up the New Year's calendar and invite participants to hold up their New Year's calendars.)* Lord God of all creation, you have given us life and permitted us to reach this new year. You bless us with many good things and hold out for us the promise of more to come. As we begin living 19__, be with us; guide and protect us through good times and bad, through sickness and health. Bless this new year. May it be for us all that you wish it to be. May we see in it all that is good and holy. Bless this new year and bless us in the name of Jesus, your Son and our brother.

All   Amen.
             (Calendars and participants may be sprinkled with holy water.)

Closing Prayer
Leader   Creator, God,
             as we begin this year, we pray anew:
             Forgive our forgettings.
             Melt our hostilities.
             Give us the courage to begin again.
             Make our memories stronger
             that we might forget less.
             Forgive more.
             Grow in relationships.
             Reach out further.
             Show our care.
             Hurry less.
             Take the time to do those things
             that count the most.

Help us remember
    that we need to do this
    especially with those who are dearest:
    families
    friends
    neighbors
    those who shape our lives and our days.
Keep us peaceful and just
    kind and compassionate
    gentle and generous
    filled with the Light of your love.

All   Amen.

Closing Song

Feast of St. Blaise
(February 3)

Blessing of Throats

Materials Needed
Lighted candles, a Bible, 2 candles attached in the form of a cross to be used for the blessing of throats.

Preparation and Environment
Gather participants in a space where each can be easily reached for blessing of throats. On a table or altar, have lighted candles, a Bible, and the candles to be used for blessing of throats.

Introduction
Today we remember St. Blaise, a bishop in Armenia in the fourth century. Legend tells us that Blaise was a doctor before he became a bishop. He healed a young boy who was choking on a fish bone. For this reason, he has been venerated as a patron of those who suffer from diseases of the throat. It is a custom to have our throats blessed on his feast day. The blessing of St. Blaise is a sign of our faith in God's protection and love for us and for the sick.

Opening Prayer
Leader Gracious God, we rejoice in the glory of your saints. In your loving kindness, grant your people protection and grace. Give them health of mind and body, and make them always faithful to you. Amen.

Scripture Reading
Luke 4:38–40

Response
"Alleluia" *(sung)*

Intercessions
Leader The Lord is good and listens to our prayers. Let us pray for those in need of God's healing: For those who suffer from sickness, let us pray to the Lord.

All Lord, have mercy.

Leader For those suffering from sadness and depression, let us pray to the Lord.

All Lord, have mercy.

Leader For doctors, nurses, and all who care for the sick, let us pray to the Lord.

All Lord, have mercy.

Leader For those who seek the blessing of St. Blaise today. May they be protected from afflictions of the throat and other forms of illness, let us pray to the Lord.

All Lord, have mercy.

Leader In confidence, we pray: Our Father...

Prayer of Blessing
(The leader and other ministers touch the throats of each person with the crossed candles and pray:) Through the intercession of St. Blaise, bishop and martyr, may God deliver you from every disease of the throat and from every other illness.

All Amen.

Concluding Prayer
Be with us, loving God. Keep us healthy through this winter, in the name of the Father, and of the Son, and of the Holy Spirit. Amen.

Closing Song

St. Valentine's Day

Materials Needed
Tables for participants to gather around. In the center of each table have a paper heart (at least 6 inches by 6 inches) and pens or pencils for each participant, a Bible, heart-shaped cookies, and hot cocoa or tea for sharing after the prayer.

Preparation and Environment
Gather participants around tables.

Introduction
Remind participants that this is the feast of St. Valentine, patron of lovers and sweethearts. Help them recall the giving and receiving of Valentines, inquiring whether there was a very special or favorite Valentine they remember receiving or sending.

Opening Prayer
Leader   On this feast of love, let us pray to our God who is love. *(Sign of the Cross)*
Loving God, your love is like the sun,
   warming our hearts and giving us joy.
Grant us the joy of being loved,
   and warm our hearts to love in return.

Opening Song
"You Are My Sunshine" (refrain only)

Scripture
Adapted from I John 4:7–19
(Tell the participants that there will be a response during this reading. Invite them to repeat after you:)

Leader   Love one another, for love is of God.

All   Love one another, for love is of God.

Leader   My dear people, let us love one another, for God is love and love comes from God. Love one another, for love is of God.

All   Love one another, for love is of God.

Leader God loved the world so much, he sent his only son, that all who believe in him might have eternal life. Love one another, for love is of God.

All Love one another, for love is of God.

Leader Since God has loved us, let us therefore love one another. If we love one another, God will love us and live in us in perfect love. Love one another, for love is of God.

All Love one another, for love is of God.

Leader Let not your hearts be troubled, for love has no room for fear. In love all fear is forgotten, for God is here with us. Love one another, for love is of God.

All Love one another, for love is of God.

Leader God is love, and they who abide in love, abide in God, and God in them. Love one another, for love is of God.

All Love one another, for love is of God.

Litany of Love
(Invite participants to pray for those they love. Conclude the litany with the refrain of "You Are My Sunshine.")

Ritual Action
(Invite the participants to write the names of those they love on the paper hearts. [Some may need help with this.] When all have finished, have them hold the paper heart to their hearts while singing the refrain of "You Are My Sunshine"—or the whole song if memory warrants.)

Concluding Prayer
Leader Loving God, you created the world in love
    and open the doors that lead to your love.
Let our love be love that is visible.
Let it shine in our speech,
    in our eyes,
    in our silence,
    in our deeds,
    in our whole being.

All Amen.

Gesture of Friendship
All share a snack of heart-shaped cookies and cocoa or tea.

Mardi Gras

If possible, this ritual might be celebrated in the dining room, just prior to the main meal. The meal should be sumptuous and include table cloths, candles, cloth napkins, champagne and/or non-alcoholic champagne. If it is not possible to celebrate this ritual before the main meal, it may be followed by a sharing of donuts and champagne and/or non-alcoholic champagne.

Materials Needed
An Alleluia banner, a box in which to "bury" the banner

Introduction
Leader On this eve of Ash Wednesday, we celebrate the feast of Mardi Gras, or Shrove Tuesday. By ancient custom, it is a celebration of eating, drinking and festivity in preparation for the Lenten season. In celebration of Mardi Gras, we will share with one another a pre-Lenten feast. Also by ancient custom, the Alleluia is not spoken or sung during Lent. As part of this ritual, we will "bury" our Alleluia banner until Easter. Then, in joy, we will resurrect it and display it in a special place of honor for the season.

Opening Song
"Alleluia"

Opening Prayer
Leader Lord our God, on this eve of Ash Wednesday, we ask that you bless our celebration and our feast.

All Alleluia! *(sung)*

Leader Bless our table, our food and our wine. Bless all of us who sit about this feastday table as well.

All Alleluia! *(sung)*

Leader Join us, Gracious God, at this feast, as we prepare to join your Son, Jesus, in our prayerful entry into the forty days of Lent.

All Alleluia! *(sung)*

Leader As the food and wine of this feast give nourishment and strength to our bodies and spirits, may we, during this coming season of Lent, give support and strength to each other.

All Alleluia! *(sung)*

Leader As we travel this lenten Journey, reflecting on the death of our Lord, may we also remember his victory over death, in his resurrection.

All Alleluia! *(sung)*

Leader May this dinner, on the eve of the day of ashes, be a joyful foretaste of the rebirth and new life that is promised in the feast of the resurrection.

All Alleluia! *(sung)*

Leader As we prepare to begin our Mardi Gras feast, let us toast and sing the ancient song of joy.

All "Alleluia" *(sung with glasses raised)*

After Dinner Ritual

Leader Having feasted with festivity on this eve of Lent, let us sing our "Alleluia" one last time before these forty days of Lent and then "bury it" until Easter.

(The Alleluia banner is taken down, placed in a box and covered with a purple cloth. If possible, keep the cloth-covered box in the chapel or other public place during Lent.)

Blessing of St. Joseph's Table

It is an Italian custom to celebrate the feast of St. Joseph [March 19] with a festive meal. It is customary to set a plate at the table for St. Joseph at these meals and heap it high with food, which is later given to the poor. If possible, prior to this ritual, residents might be involved in making large batches of soup and homemade bread. These can be the food for St. Joseph's plate and after the blessing can be brought to a local homeless shelter or soup kitchen.

Materials Needed
St. Joseph's plate at each table containing a large bowl of soup and a loaf of bread.

Preparation and Environment
Celebrate this blessing as a meal prayer. Explain the Italian custom.

Blessing Prayer

Leader Today we remember St. Joseph, husband of our Blessed Mother, Mary, and father-protector of the Holy Family in Nazareth. In his honor we bless these tables and this food.
Let us pray: St. Joseph, you who are the patron saint of workers, a happy death, the universal church, and every Christian home, watch over this, our home, with loving care. St. Joseph, pray for us.

All St. Joseph, pray for us.

Leader Lord, God of all creation, you who gave bread to Moses and his people while they traveled in the desert, come now, and bless these gifts of food which you have given us.

All Bless these gifts of food which you have given us.

Leader (*Invite all to extend a hand over the St. Joseph plate on their table and have one person at each table hold up the loaf of bread.*) St. Joseph, may this food, created in your honor, be not only a cause of celebration for us. May it also be nourishment for us and those with whom we share this soup and bread. May it and your intercession sustain us so that at the end of our days we will be blessed with a happy death. Bless this food and us.

All Bless this food and bless us.

Leader St. Joseph, we give you honor, today as we ask the blessing of God, the Father, the Son, and the Holy Spirit, upon this food and upon us.

All Amen.

Feasts of Mary

This service can be adapted for any of the Marian feasts during the year.

Materials Needed
A statue or picture of Mary, a rosary, flowers, other appropriate symbols for the day.

Introduction
Today we celebrate the_____ feast of Mary.
(Comment briefly on the particular feast.)
Let us honor her in prayer and song.

Opening Song
A familiar Marian hymn

Opening Prayer
Mother, Mary, in Christ we are your children, and we pray: Hail Mary, full of grace...

Scripture Reading
Gospel of the day or other appropriate Scripture

Response
Alleluia   *(sung or spoken)*

Mary's Prayer
(On the feast of the Visitation, this could serve as the Scripture Reading.)

Leader   My soul magnifies the Lord.

All   My soul magnifies the Lord.

Leader   My soul magnifies the Lord.
      and my spirit rejoices in God my savior,
      for he has looked with favor
      on the lowliness of his servant.
My soul magnifies the Lord.

All   My soul magnifies the Lord.

Leader   Surely, from now on

all generations will call me blessed;
for the Mighty One has done great things for me,
and holy is his name.
My soul magnifies the Lord.

All   My soul magnifies the Lord.

Leader   His mercy is for those who fear him
from generation to generation.
He has shown strength with his arm;
he has scattered the proud
in the thoughts of their hearts.
My soul magnifies the Lord.

All   My soul magnifies the Lord.

Leader   He has brought down the powerful from their thrones,
and lifted up the lowly;
he has filled the hungry with good things,
and sent the rich away empty.
My soul magnifies the Lord.

All   My soul magnifies the Lord.

Leader   He has helped his servant Israel,
in a remembrance of his mercy,
according to the promise he made to our ancestors,
to Abraham and to his descendants forever.
My soul magnifies the Lord.

All   My soul magnifies the Lord.

Hymn

Closing Prayer (from the Litany of Loreto)
Leader   Let us pray: Lord, have mercy.

All   Lord, have mercy.

Leader   Christ, have mercy.

All   Christ, have mercy.

Leader   Lord, have mercy.

All   Lord, have mercy.

Leader   Holy Mary,

All   *(after each invocation)* Pray for us.

Leader   Holy Mother of God,
Sinless Mother,
Ark of the covenant,
Health of the sick,
Refuge of sinners,
Comfort of the troubled,
Cause of all joy,
Help of Christians,
Queen of all saints,
Queen of peace,

Leader   Pray for us, holy Mother of God.

Closing Song
(A familiar Marian hymn)

Feast of Angels
(September 29)

Materials Needed

An "Angel-on-my-shoulder pin" for each participant

Introduction

Today is the feast of the Archangels *(inquire whether anyone remembers who they are)*: Michael, Gabriel, Raphael.

The word angel means "messenger" and in Scripture that is what they do. They deliver God's message and then disappear. They plant the seed, let others tend it, and take no credit, for the message comes from God.

Opening Prayer

Leader   Loving God, in a wonderful way you guide the work of angels and people. May those who serve you constantly in heaven keep our lives safe from all harm on earth. We ask this through Jesus Christ, your Son and our brother.

All   Amen.

Scripture

Revelation 12:7–9

Psalm Response

Psalm 138:1–2, 3–4, 4–5

(Response between each verse: In the sight of the angels we will sing your praises, Lord.)

Scripture

Luke 1:26–28

Homily

Spend some time talking with participants about angels. Ask if anyone remembers the traditional Guardian Angel Prayer:

Angel of God, my guardian dear,
   to whom God's love commits me here,
   ever this day, be at my side,
   to light to guard, to rule and guide. Amen.

Angels are sent by God to do God's will. They are naturally good. If someone says "You're an angel," it is, indeed, a compliment.

Intercessions

Leader   Let us pray for all those "angels" that have been part of our lives.
(All respond "Lord, hear our prayer" to each intercession. Conclude the Intercessions with the traditional Guardian Angel prayer.)

Ritual Action

Leader   There have been many who have been "angels" in our lives. And each of us have been, and are, "angels" for others. As a reminder that we are to be God's messengers and do God's will, receive this small angel pin.
(Pin an "angel" on each participant, as you say, "N., you're an angel.")

Concluding Prayer

Leader   Loving God, in venerating your faithful angels and archangels we also praise your glory, for in honoring them, we honor you, their creator. Their splendor shows us your greatness. May we learn from them to always do your will and be your messengers of Good News.

All   Amen.

St. Nicholas Day
(December 6)

Materials Needed
A candy cane for each participant

Background
Nicholas was a kindly and popular bishop who lived in the fourth century. He was known for generously taking care of orphans, giving dowries to poor servant girls, dropping money down chimneys of poor families, leaving food outside the doors of hungry people. Although he tried to perform his acts of kindness in secret, he still became known for his charity. After his death, his kindnesses became legend in the minds and hearts of the needy. When he was declared a saint, his feast day was set on December 6, and the day became an occasion for gift-giving.

Introduction

Leader *(Ask participants: Did you ever celebrate St. Nicholas Day in your family? What did you do?)* Today is the Feast of St. Nicholas. Let us pray in honor of his feast and his compassion. Please respond "Grant us your blessing, great-hearted one" after each prayer.

Leader Good St. Nicholas, patron and holy symbol of joy for many people of many lands, we honor you on this your feast day.

All Grant us your blessing, great-hearted one.

Leader Be our companion as we once again prepare our home and hearts for the miracle of the coming of Emmanuel.

All Grant us your blessing, great-hearted one.

Leader *(holding up some candy canes)* May these candy canes, shaped like your bishop's staff, be for us a sign of your benevolent care and a reminder to us of the care that we give and receive.

All Grant us your blessing, great-hearted one.

Leader We rejoice that you are the holy bringer of gifts and that so many have been delighted by your great generosity. Help us be as generous of heart.

All Grant us your blessing, great-hearted one.

Leader Wherever these candy canes are hung on tree, wall, or door, may they carry with them the bright blessing of God.

All Grant us your blessing, great-hearted one.

Leader May all who taste these candy canes experience the sweetness of God on their tongues and in their hearts; and may they be a sign of Advent joy for us.

All Grant us your blessing, great-hearted one.

Leader When, in our day-to-day lives we become anxious, weary, and in need of strength, may these canes be a sign of the support we receive.

All Grant us your blessing, great-hearted one.

Leader And most of all, jolly saint of gifts and sweets, help us stay youthful, humorous, playful, and dream-filled as we journey together toward the future.

All Grant us your blessing, great-hearted one.

Ritual Action
Give each participant a candy cane and invite them to hang it somewhere in their rooms as a reminder of St. Nicholas and his kindness and generosity.

Celebratory Days
and Special Occasions

A Birthday or Anniversary Ritual

This ritual can be adapted and used for the celebration of a couple's anniversary.

Material Needed
Table for participants to gather around with a specially decorated place for the celebrant, a decorated birthday cake, a candle, party hats for everyone

Preparation and Environment
Gather participants around the table. If necessary help them put on the party hats.

Introduction
Greetings and introduction of the resident who is celebrating a birthday. Explain that this gathering is to pray with and for the celebrant and bestow a special blessing upon them.

Opening Prayer
Leader   Lord of Life,
>we gather today to celebrate the day
>when N. was born
>and became a gift to her/his parents
>and to the world.

We thank you for giving us N.
>for she/he is a gift to us as well.

And we thank you for her/his _____ years of life.
Thank you, Lord, for giving us N.

All   Thank you, Lord, for giving us N.

Scripture
(from Isaiah 43)
Thus says Yahweh, who created you and formed you:
Do not be afraid, for I am your God.
You are precious in my eyes.
You are honored and I love you.

Ritual Action
The celebrant is invited to light the birthday candle and share with the group her/his story of life. Note: Some residents may need prompting questions.

When the story is finished, the leader says:

Leader   Thank you, Lord, for giving us N.

All   Thank you, Lord, for giving us N.

Blessing
Invite more mobile residents, family members, and staff to gather around the cele-brant and place their hands on her/his head, shoulders, arms and hands.

Leader   Lord of Birthdays and Festivals,
    send your blessing on N. today.
May she/he grow younger with each birthday,
May the gifts of this day
    be the blessing of good health,
    peaceful days,
    and the joys of family and friends.
Happy birthday, N.
May God bless you today
    and all the days of your life.

Gesture of Friendship
All sing "Happy Birthday" and enjoy cake and ice cream.

Civic Holidays

This service can be adapted for use on various civic holidays (Independence Day, Flag Day, Veterans Day, President's Day, Election Day, etc.). It can also be adapted for World and National needs. See Lectionary readings for Masses for Civil and Public Needs for optional Scriptures.

Materials Needed
A small flag for each participant, a recording of patriotic, John Philip Sousa-type music to be played before and after the service for toe-tapping, hum-along, and flag waving. Other appropriate holiday symbols: pictures of Washington and Lincoln for President's Day, etc.

Introduction
Today is _____ Day.
(Comment briefly about the particular holiday.)

Opening Song
"Come, Holy Ghost"

Opening Prayer

Leader   Father of heaven and earth, hear our prayer and show us the way to peace in the world. Lord, have mercy.

All   Lord, have mercy.

Leader   Christ, have mercy.

All   Christ, have mercy.

Leader   Lord, have mercy.

All   Lord, have mercy.

First Reading
Isaiah 32:15–20

Psalm Response
Psalm 85:10, 11–12, 13–14
Sung response: "The Lord speaks of peace to the people."

Second Reading
Colossians 3:12–15

Alleluia Verse *(sung)*
Alleluia, Alleluia, Alleluia!
Peace I leave with you. My peace I give to you.
Alleluia, Alleluia, Alleluia!

Gospel Reading
John 20:19–23

Homily

Intercessory Prayers
Leader   Let us pray for the needs of our country and for our own needs.
For our church, city, state and national leaders. May they be strengthened by the Holy Spirit as they lead God's people....Let us pray to the Lord.

All   Lord, hear our prayer.

Leader   Protect, O saving God, the city in which we live and all of its people.

All   Lord, hear our prayer.

Leader   Bless, loving God, all citizens of our country. Keep us all safe and give us peace.

All   Lord, hear our prayer.
(Invite participants for offer intercessory prayers.)

Leader   Gathering our prayers and petitions, let us now offer the prayer that Jesus taught us. Our Father...

Closing Prayer
Leader   We give you thanks and praise, O God. Fill us with your Spirit and help us live in peace and love. We make this prayer in Jesus' name.

All   Amen.

Closing Song
"America the Beautiful"

Celebrating Caregivers

This ritual might be celebrated during National Nursing Home Week or some other appropriate time. It is advisable that as many employees of the facility as possible be present for the ritual.

Materials Needed

A candle, several small bowls of scented oil, a copy of the Prayer of Caregivers for each staff person.

Introduction

Leader   Today we celebrate and give thanks for all those who care for us each and every day. *(Light the candle.)*   Let us remember that we are in the holy presence of God.

Opening Reflection

"A Shut-in's Prayer"

Leader or Resident

> You and I, Lord,
> > we share a secret.
>
> Sometimes it's tempting
> > to give in to the sympathy,
> > all those well-meant words:
>
> "You poor thing. You must get terribly lonesome."
> "You're just a living saint, my dear."
> "It's an inspiration the way you bear all your sufferings."
>
> Do you see what I mean, Lord?
> It's tempting.
> But you and I share a secret.
> You once said,
> > "You will not enter the Kingdom of Heaven
> > unless you become like a little child."
>
> Well, I'm getting there, Lord.
> My circle of friends and acquaintances
> > has dwindled considerably.
>
> But you, Lord, are considerate
> > enough to fill the gap.

I can't even cross the street by myself.
But take my hand, Lord,
    and I'll bear that cross.
Since I don't do anything,
    I don't do anything wrong.
But you know everything, Lord,
    so you know better!
I'm depending more and more on others.
Thank you, Lord, more and more
    for the others who are your church.

You and I, Lord,
    we share a secret.
Lean down here and let me
    whisper in your ear.
Look at my loneliness, my lack of mobility,
    my time-set ways, all my aches and pains.
For whatever good they may do,
    I accept and offer these "gifts"
    for the sake of those
    people who search
    for what I already possess.
Fill the beakers of their loneliness
    with the sweet fellowship
    of your church.
Lead them by the hand on their crossing
    to faith.
Teach them that when they reach out to others
    they touch you.
Welcome them warmly
    into the communion of saints.
Finally, grant them a share
    in your own suffering,
    and thus a portion
    in the Kingdom to come.

And me, Lord?
I'll stay right here,
    watching and waiting, praying for them,
    keeping my mouth shut,
    my heart and mind open.
And if it's all right with you, we'll just
    let all this be our little secret.

Ah, but you know me, Lord.
I'm liable to tell everyone I know!*

Brief Time for Reflection

Scripture
Luke 13:10–13

Litany of Thanks

Leader For those who give us understanding and love,

All We thank you, Lord.

Leader For those who are there when we are in need of assistance,

All We thank you, Lord.

Leader For those who help us find answers to doubts,

All We thank you, Lord.

Leader For those who understand our suffering and pain,

All We thank you, Lord.

Leader For those who confront wisely the problems we face,

All We thank you, Lord.

Leader For those who pray with us,

All We thank you, Lord.

Leader For those who are patient and clear-minded,

All We thank you, Lord.

Leader For those who give comfort when we are in darkness and despair,

All We thank you, Lord.

(*from *Bright Intervals* [James Bitney, Winston Press, Minneapolis MN, 1982] used with permission of the author)

Leader   For those whose help never fails,

All   We thank you, Lord.

Leader   For those who provide administration here,

All   We thank you, Lord.

Leader   For those who heal our ills,

All   We thank you, Lord.

Leader   For those who bathe us and clean our clothes and our rooms,

All   We thank you, Lord.

Leader   For those who alleviate pain with gentle hands,

All   We thank you, Lord.

Leader   For those who feed our hunger,

All   We thank you, Lord.

Leader   For those who bring delight to our days with companionship and activities,

All   We thank you, Lord.

Leader   For those who visit and bring joy,

All   We thank you, Lord.
   (Invite participants to offer prayers for specific caregivers who have been special to them.)

Blessing of Caregivers

Leader   Let us now ask God to bless these special people in our lives. And since blessings come from God through people, I invite you all to extend a hand in blessing as we pray.

   Let us pray: Lord God, in your loving kindness you have given us these compassionate caregivers. Let your Spirit uphold and strengthen them always as they exercise their ministry of care.
   (Residents take bowls of scented oil and anoint caregivers by tracing a sign of the cross on their foreheads or hands.)

Prayer of Caregivers

Help us, loving God, to receive with honor, respect, understanding, and love, all those who seek us and are in need of assistance. Teach us understanding and empathy, gentleness and mercy. May your inspiration guide us as we strive to be your servants. Grant us unselfishness and humility that we may always be there for those we serve, and touch them with love and compassion. Amen.

Closing Song

(appropriate Thanksgiving hymn)

Celebrating the Seasons

This ritual is designed to help welcome the beginnings of Spring (March 21), Summer (June 21), Autumn (September 21), and Winter (December 21). The same format may be used for each celebration, with the appropriate seasonal prayers inserted where indicated. It would be appropriate to conclude each ritual with a sharing of seasonal fruits and wine or grape juice, to toast the new season.

Materials Needed
Candles of appropriate color for each solstice, symbols appropriate to each season (Spring branches and flowers, Autumn leaves, etc.)

Gathering
Leader Today is the first day of _____, the day we celebrate the _____ solstice. Our ancient ancestors traditionally celebrated the solstices around seasonal fires. For this reason, it is appropriate that we light this seasonal candle, welcome _____, and thank God for this new season.

Blessed are you Lord, God of all Creation,
    you filled the world with wonderful things,
    and gave nature many faces for us to enjoy.
Blessed are you Lord, God of all Creation,
    you give us the rich variety
    of ever-changing seasons.

Scripture
Psalm 148 (adapted)
(All respond "Bless the Lord" after each invocation.)

Bless the Lord, all you things the Lord has made,
    praise and exalt God forever.
Sun and moon,
Stars of heaven,
Waters above the heavens,
Waters below the heavens,
Every shower and rainbow,
All you winds,
Fire and heat,
Cold and chill,
Dew and rain,

Frost and cold,
Ice and snow,
Nights and days,
Light and darkness,
Lightning and clouds,
Mountains and hills,
Everything growing from the earth,
Seas and rivers,
Beasts wild and tame,
Sea creatures and birds,
Winter and Summer,
Autumn and Spring,
Let everything that has breath bless the Lord.

All   Glory be the Father, and to the Son, and to the Holy Spirit, as it was in the beginning, is now and ever shall be, world without end. Amen.

Seasonal Greeting
(See below.)

Opening Song
(appropriate seasonal song)

Seasonal Prayer of Welcome
(See below.)

Ritual Action
Toast the new season with a glass of wine and enjoy the seasonal fruit. Each participant is given a seasonal symbol.

Closing Prayer
(See below.)

Closing Song
"Canticle of the Sun"*

* Marty Haugen, GIA Publications, Inc. 7404 S. Mason Ave., Chicago IL 60638

Spring

Greeting

Leader   Awake, all you seeds of the earth,
       buried in dark earthen tombs.
As this flame of our candle
       lights the darkness,
       may your tender shoots spring forth
       to dance in wind, rain, and sun,
       just as this flame now dances before us.

Prayer of Welcome

Leader   Lord, God of all Creation,
       with spring there is hope,
       carried upon the wind,
       filling field and forest, city and town.
We welcome you, season of spring.

All   We welcome you, season of spring.

Leader   Lord, God of all Creation,
       with joy, we welcome the spring sun
       which warms and feeds our earth with energy and light.
We welcome you, season of spring.

All   We welcome you, season of spring.

Leader   Lord, God of all Creation,
       teach us the lesson of spring,
       that all creation comes alive—
       trees and bushes, flowers and plants—
We welcome you, season of spring.

All   We welcome you, season of spring.

Leader   In the alleluia of new life
       and the resurrection of all creation, we sing

All   Alleluia *(sung)*

Closing Prayer

Leader Lord God of all Creation,
        teach us, in this glorious season of spring,
        the lesson that nothing dies completely.
    At the death of our bodies help us to know
        that we have not entered an endless winter,
        but simply a stage in the unfolding mystery of life.
    May we taste with delight
        the freshness and vitality of new birth
        and come forth from the long winter
        joyful and fully alive
        in the presence of God.

Summer

Greeting

Leader Holy is this flame of midsummer,
      and holy are you O, God,
      who from your heart
      comes love and life.

Prayer of Welcome

Leader Lord, God of all Creation,
      with summer there are sun-drenched flowers, food and drink.
      With joy we welcome the summer sun.
      We welcome you, season of summer.

All   We welcome you, season of summer.

Leader This food we are about to share
      is sun-kissed and full of life.
      May we eat and drink these gifts
      in your company while giving you thanks.
      We welcome you, season of summer.

All   We welcome you, season of summer.

Leader Bless this food and drink
      in the circle-sign of the sun,
      the holy sign of your unending love.
      We welcome you, season of summer.

All   We welcome you, season of summer.

Closing Prayer

Leader Lord, God of all creation,
      set our hearts aflame
      and our feet playfully dancing
      as we delight in the warmth of your love.
      We thank you for the sun, rain, and growth of this season.
      As we celebrate this magical season
      open our eyes to the countless wonders
      that you have planted in each of us.

Autumn

Greeting

Leader O flame of autumn color,
     speak to us, as the earth begins to cool,
     of the promise hidden in this season.
  We welcome you, Autumn, with arms full of summer's blessings,
     fruits, vegetables, and seeds of life for next year's planting.

Prayer of Welcome

Leader Lord, God of all Creation,
     our life is a feast overflowing
     with the delights of your harvest.
  We welcome you, season of autumn.

All   We welcome you, season of autumn.

Leader We rejoice in the delights of your gifts.
  In thanksgiving we glory in the fresh taste,
     touch and sight of this season.
  We welcome you, season of autumn.

All   We welcome you, season of autumn.

Leader We greet you, seeds of the season
     carrying life for next year's planting.
  We welcome you, season of autumn.

All   We welcome you, season of autumn.

Closing Prayer

Leader Lord, God of all Creation,
     great and generous are you.
  Our life is a feast
     that overflows with the delights of your presence.
  Teach us in this glorious season of Autumn,
     to sing a neverending song of thanks.

Winter

Greeting

Leader We stand at the threshold of Christmas.
May today's celebration be in harmony with that most holy day.
May it help us truly rejoice in the birth of the Light of the World.
May our Winter solstice also be celebrated
in union with our Jewish sisters and brothers,
who in this time of darkness
celebrate Hanukkah, their holy feast of light.

Prayer of Welcome

Leader Lord, God of all Creation,
darkness leans over us this winter season.
May we find hope in the lights we kindle.
May we find hope in one another
and all who perform the care we receive.
We welcome you, season of winter.

All We welcome you, season of winter.

Leader May the joys of this winter season
brighten our spirits and warm our hearts
with a taste of promised peace on earth.
We welcome you, season of winter.

All We welcome you, season of winter.

Leader May this food and drink we share be blessed—
a winter solstice toast to the sun and snow of this season.
We welcome you, season of winter.

All We welcome you, season of winter.

Closing Prayer

Leader May we who celebrate this winter season
be mindful of the darkness of hate and greed,
of war and discrimination.
May we find hope in one another and
call forth the prayer and love of each other.

Communal Reconciliation Service

Materials Needed
A large pearl for each participant

Greeting
Leader   We gather today in joy knowing that we are a forgiven and forgiving people. We gather to give thanks and praise to God, who has made us fit to share in the inheritance of the holy ones; for God delivered us from the power of darkness through his Son, Jesus, in whom we have redemption and forgiveness of sin.

Opening Song

Opening Prayer
Leader   May the grace and peace of God our Father be with you.

All   And also with you.

Leader   Let us pray:
Merciful God, you bring us the good news
    that you are a God who forgives.
Carry this good news
    to all who strive to celebrate your loving mercy.
Through your bountiful goodness
    pardon our offenses and
    free us from the sins we have committed in our frailty.
Give us hearts of flesh,
    hearts big enough to welcome you into our lives
    with joy, praise, and thanksgiving,
    through Christ, our Lord.

All   Amen.

Scripture
Ephesians 1:3–7

Response
Psalm 103:1–5, 8–12

Leader   The Lord is tender and caring.

All   The Lord is tender and caring.

Leader My soul, bless the Lord,
bless God's holy name!
My soul, bless the Lord,
hold dear all God's gifts!

All The Lord is tender and caring.

Leader Bless God, who forgives your sin
and heals every illness,
who snatches you from death
and enfolds you with tender care,
who fills your life with richness
and gives you an eagle's strength.

All The Lord is tender and caring.

Leader The Lord is tender and caring,
slow to anger, rich in love.
God will not accuse us long,
nor bring our sins to trial,
nor exact from us in kind
what our sins deserve.

All The Lord is tender and caring.

Leader As high as heaven above earth,
so great is God's love for believers.
As far as east from west,
so God removes our sins.

All The Lord is tender and caring.

Gospel Acclamation
Alleluia *(sung)*

Scripture
Matthew 13:44–46

Homily

Litany of Sorrow
Leader With sorrow for taking God's goodness and kindness for granted,
we pray to the Lord,

All Lord, have mercy.

Leader For failing to love as we are commanded,
  we pray to the Lord,

All Lord, have mercy.

Leader For neglecting to respond to God's grace and inspiration,
  we pray to the Lord,

All Lord, have mercy.

Leader For not responding to those in need,
  we pray to the Lord,

All Lord, have mercy.

Leader For giving in to pride and self-pity,
  we pray to the Lord,

All Lord, have mercy.

Leader For misusing the beauty and resources of the earth,
  we pray to the Lord,

All Lord, have mercy.

Leader For all our deliberate sins,
  we pray to the Lord,

All Lord, have mercy.

Leader For not giving thanks every day of our lives,
  we pray to the Lord,

All Lord, have mercy.

Leader May God have mercy on us, forgive all our sins, and bring us to everlasting life.

All Amen.

Examination of Conscience and Confession of Sins

Leader Let us now examine our consciences, and confess our sinfulness to God.

Leader Loving God, you welcome us as wayward children,
  you rejoice at our return

like the finder of a long-lost coin or perfect pearl.
For our sake you risked all, sold all,
   and purchased us at great price.
Your generosity overwhelms us.
Bless us, merciful God.
Bring us to see you eye to eye, face to face.
And remind us of your amazing promise,
      that your forgiveness is always ours,
         through Christ Jesus, our Lord and Savior.

All   Amen.

Ritual Action

Participants are invited to approach the leader and other ministers. If they wish, they may mention a sin for which they are particularly sorry, or they may simply come in silence. As they come forward, the ministers lay hands on them and say, "God rejoices in your repentance, for you are a Pearl of Great Price."

They then give each participant a large pearl. During this ritual action, appropriate hymns may be sung or instrumental music may be played.

Absolution

Leader   Those who wish to receive the sacramental absolution of the church, please bow your heads.

May God give you pardon and peace
   in the knowledge that we walk in the Light of Christ.
Through the ministry of the church,
   God has taken from us everything that cannot bear this light.
And through the ministry of that same church,
   I absolve you from your sins,
      in the name of the Father, and of the Son, and of the Holy Spirit.

All   Amen.

Concluding Prayer

Leader   Gracious God, by baptism and reconciliation, you have called us to be your light to the world. Let this good work shine forth in us, so that all may glorify you. Go forth, People of Light, God's Pearls of Great Price, in the peace and joy of the Lord.

All   Thanks be to God.
(All exchange a sign of peace.)

Concluding Song

Memorial Service

Note: This service might be celebrated once a year, twice a year, or more often depending on the facility and the number of deaths that occur. It is designed to be used either within or outside a Eucharistic Celebration. Scripture texts from the Order of Christian Funerals may be substituted for those suggested. Staff members, caregivers, and family members of the deceased may be invited to participate in this service. After the service, all may be invited to share refreshments.

Materials Needed

Bible, a candle for each person who has died, burning charcoal and incense grains, Memory Book, a bouquet of roses, carnations, or daisies—one flower for each person being remembered.

Welcome

As we celebrate this memorial service together we hope you may find space to remember, to grieve, to be comforted, and to find hope.

Greeting

Leader Praised be God our Father, who raised Jesus Christ from the dead. Blessed be God forever.

All Blessed be God forever.

Leader Today is a day of memories for us, as we pause to recall those friends who have died in the past____ months. They have passed from life with us to new life with Christ in the company of God's saints.
(Each person is named and a candle is lighted. Family members may be invited to light candles if they are present. Soft music may be played at this time.)

Prayer

Leader Blessed are you, Lord our God,
　　keeper of the Book of Life.
Today we remember and pray
　　for those friends and family members
　　who have passed through the doorway of death.
We remember and pray, too, for their families.
Support them in their loss with the consolation of your Holy Spirit.
We pray for ourselves as well.
May their death be for us a holy message
　　of how not to waste our todays,
　　or be unprepared for the arrival of our own deaths.

May we best remember those who have gone before us
    by being grateful for life today
    and by loving you, Lord our God,
    keeper of the Book of Life.

Scripture
1 Thessalonians 4:13–18

Response
Alleluia *(sung)*

Scripture
John 14:1–6

Response
Alleluia *(sung)*

Intercessions

Leader   God, the Almighty Father, raised Christ, his Son, from the dead;
    with confidence we ask God to save all people, living and dead.
For all of our loved ones,
    in baptism they were given the pledge of eternal life.
May they now enjoy the company of the saints.
We pray to the Lord.

All   Lord, hear our prayer.

Leader   For all of our loved ones,
    in Eucharist they received the body of Christ, the bread of life.
May they be raised up on the last day.
We pray to the Lord.

All   Lord, hear our prayer.

Leader   For all our loved ones
    who have lost family members and friends.
May they be consoled in their grief by the Lord
    who wept at the death of his friend Lazarus.
We pray to the Lord.

All   Lord, hear our prayer.

Leader   For all our loved ones
    who have gone before us.

May they have the reward of their goodness.
We pray to the Lord.

All   Lord, hear our prayer.

Leader   For all gathered here today
        to remember, give thanks, and celebrate the lives of loved ones.
May they know the Lord's strength and consolation
We pray to the Lord.

All   Lord, hear our prayer.

Leader   God, our shelter and our strength, you listen in love to the cry of your people. Hear the prayers we offer on behalf of those we love.

Litany of Remembrance

(Each name from the Memory Book is read, along with the date of death. After each name, a couple of grains of incense are placed on the burning charcoal.)

Leader   With Christ there is mercy and fullness of redemption; let us remember our friends who have died. As long as we live, they, too, will live. For they are now a part of us as we remember them.
(All respond after each invocation, "We remember them.")
At the rising of the sun and at its going down…
At the blowing of the wind and in the chill of winter…
At the opening of the buds and in the rebirth of spring…
At the blueness of the skies and in the warmth of summer…
At the rustling of the leaves and in the beauty of autumn…
At the beginning of the year and when it ends…
As long as we live, they, too, will live.
For they are now a part of us as we remember them.

For all the good they've done…
For the wisdom they imparted…
For the faith and hope they shared…
For the stories they told…
For the love they poured out…
As long as we live, they, too, will live.
For they are now a part of us as we remember them.

When we are weary and in need of strength…
When we are lost and sick at heart…
When we have a joy we crave to share…
When we have decisions that are difficult to make…

When we have achievements that are based on theirs...
As long as we live, they, too, will live.
For they are now a part of us as we remember them.

Prayer

Leader All-powerful God,
    whose mercy is never withheld
    from those who call upon you in hope,
    look kindly on your servants
    and number them among your saints for evermore.
We ask this through Christ our Lord.

All Amen.

Leader Eternal rest grant unto them, O Lord.

All And let perpetual light shine upon them.

Leader May they rest in peace.

All Amen.

Leader May their souls and the souls of all the faithful departed, through the mercy of God, rest in peace.

All Amen.

Blessing

Leader May the God of strength be with us, holding us in strong-fingered hands.

All Amen.

Leader May the God of compassion be with us, holding us close when we are weary, hurt, and alone.

All Amen.

Leader May Almighty God bless us, in the name of the Father, and of the Son, and of the Holy Spirit.

All Amen.

Closing Song

Memorial Rosary

The rosary is prayed in the usual manner, but in place of the mysteries, the following, or other appropriate, Scriptures and prayers are prayed to set the reflection theme for each decade.

Materials Needed

Bible, a candle for each person who has died, rosaries for any resident who does not have one.

Welcome

As we celebrate this memorial service together, we hope you may find space to remember, to grieve, to be comforted, and to find hope.

Greeting

Leader Praised be God our Father, who raised Jesus Christ from the dead. Blessed be God forever.

All Blessed be God forever.

Leader Today is a day of memories for us, as we pause to recall those friends who have died in the past____ months. They have passed from life with us to new life with Christ in the company of God's saints.
(Each person is named and a candle is lighted. Family members may be invited to light candles if they are present. Soft music may be played at this time.)

Prayer of the Rosary

First Decade
Wisdom 3:1–6

Leader Loving God, keep our loved ones in the palm of your hand. As you have filled them with your eternal joy, fill the emptiness left in our hearts by their passing with your spirit of hope.

Second Decade
Psalm 23

Leader Gracious Good Shepherd, reward your faithful ones who live with you in eternity and continue to guide those of us on earth who find it all too easy to stray.

Third Decade

Romans 8:32–35

Leader Compassionate God, help us be consoled in the knowledge that nothing can separate those we have loved from your love. And help us when our sense of hope may be dimmed.

Fourth Decade

John 11:23–26

Leader Merciful God, help us believe that Jesus is our resurrection and our life, and the source of eternal life for those whose loss we mourn.

Fifth Decade

John 14:1–3

Leader Loving God, provide that special place with you for all those we have loved, who have preceded us through the doors of death. And come back someday to take us to be with you and them for eternity.

Welcoming a New Resident

Note: If the new resident is not able to assume an active role in this ritual a family member or staff member could pray those sections with some minor adaptations. Follow this Welcome Ritual with a special luncheon or tea in honor of the new resident. Include family members, other residents, and staff members. Consider printing the Blessing Prayers for appropriate display in the resident's room.

Materials Needed
Holy water, an evergreen branch for sprinkling

Preparation and Environment
Gather in the new resident's room with staff, family members of the new resident, and residents from neighboring rooms.

Introduction
Introductions of leader and participants

Greeting
It is with joy that today we welcome N. to our community, and so we gather here in her/his room to bless N.'s new home and to bless N.

Prayer for a New Stage of Life
New Resident God, as I begin this new stage of life,
    let me retain strength of spirit.
May my life maintain its sense of purpose;
    may it continue as an example of
    faith, hope, love, and courage
    to my family and friends.

Room Blessing
Leader Let us pray:
Good and Gracious God,
    this room is to be N.'s new home.
We pray that you furnish it in peace
    and decorate it with holiness,
    so that your Sacred Presence will abide here, too.

New

Resident Lord, it is not large or grand,
        but it is to be my new home,
        a place for living, sleeping, and praying.
     May I also find within it
        refreshment, serenity, and healing.

Leader Loving God, may peace, love, and beauty
        flow out from this room in all four directions
        and up and down as well.

New

Resident May this room of mine
        be blessed by you, my God,
        as a home for me
        and for you as well. Amen.
     (A sign of the cross may be traced on the four walls and on the door of the room.)

Blessing of New Resident

Leader N., may God grant you peace and rest while you live with us.
     May your family and friends always feel welcome.
     May the time you live with us
        be filled with joy, comfort, and special warm feelings
        of friendship and care.
     May each day be filled with fond memories,
        for we treasure the gift that you are.
     May you trust in the beauty of tomorrow
        as you continue on life's journey.
     And may you succeed in enjoying the rarest gem of all,
        the making of beautiful days worth remembering.

(Invite participants to lay their hands on the head and shoulders of the new resident and/or extend a hand in blessing.)
May God bless you and keep you.
May God's face shine upon you
     and be gracious to you.
May God look upon you with kindness
     and give you peace.
And may God always hold you
     in the palm of his hand.
Amen.
(Sprinkle the room and the new resident with holy water.)

Blessing for a Sick Resident

This prayer is designed to be prayed in the room of the person who is ill. **Participants may include roommates and neighboring residents, family members and staff.**

Materials Needed

Copies of the prayer for those with leadership roles

Call to Prayer

Leader We are deeply concerned about the health of N., who is dear to us. And so we gather here at her/his bedside and commend her/his health to your care.

Scripture

Matthew 10:1

Prayer

Family or Staff Member Compassionate Lord of health and wholeness, your servant N. is sick and desires to be restored to the balance of good health. Hear our prayers for the healing of her/him whom we love so much.

All Lord, hear our prayer for N.

Roommate or Other Resident God of health and wholeness, remove this illness from N., so that fully recovered and restored to health, she/he may return with renewed zest to the daily life that we share.

All Lord, hear our prayer for N.

Resident, Family or Staff Member Loving God, we trust in your Divine Power to stir the hidden healing powers of the body. We pray that these God-given powers might remove all that causes pain and sickness in N.

All Lord, hear our prayer for N.

Health Care Provider Divine Healer, may the medicine that has been prescribed for N. heal and call forth the hidden powers of her/his body. Through the power of the Cross of Christ, may this medicine, blended with faith and devotion, restore her/him to the fullness of health.

All   Lord, hear our prayer for N.

Leader   *(addressing the sick person)*
With hope and faith, we now place our hands upon you as we call forth the healing power of God's grace.

(Persons praying may lay hands on the sick person and pray in silence for a few moments. Then, with hands still on the sick person, the Leader—or all—pray:)
Divine Healer and Lord of Wholeness,
     we ask for renewed health for N.,
Yet, we place the health of N.
     and ourselves in your hands.
Help us embrace whatever you decree for her/him.
Assist her/him in the acceptance of this illness
     as you support her/him
     with the strength of your Holy Spirit.

All   Lord, hear our prayer for N.

Leader   *(addressing the sick person)*
May you be blessed
     with the healing power and love of God,
     and the affection of those who love you.

All   Amen.
(The sick person may be signed by participants with the sign of the cross and, if appropriate, may also be kissed.)

When Someone Is Hospitalized

This prayer might be prayed as part of a regular facility Eucharist or prayer service after a resident has been hospitalized, or as a short prayer with the neighboring residents of the hospitalized resident.

Introduction
Leader Our friend N. has been taken to the hospital. In our love, care, and concern for her/him, we pray:

Prayer
Leader Compassionate God, we are deeply concerned for our friend N. Our greatest wish is that she/he might return to us in good health.

All Lord, hear our prayer.

Leader Our prayer rises from the bottom of our hearts to you the Lord of healing and wholeness.

All Lord, hear our prayer.

Leader We know that you do not rejoice in the suffering of your people. Hear our prayer that N. may soon be restored to good health.

All Lord, hear our prayer.

Leader Divine Healer, may the medicine that has been prescribed for N. and the care given her/him heal and call forth the hidden powers of her/his body. Through the power of the Cross of Christ, may this medicine, blended with faith and devotion, restore her/him to the fullness of health.

All Lord, hear our prayer.

Leader We place in your healing hands, Merciful God, our friend N. who is sick and suffering so much. Speed the happy day of recovery and return her/him to us.

All Lord, hear our prayer.

Leader We gather our prayers and offer them to God in the words that Jesus taught us. Our Father...

Thanksgiving for Improved Health
or Return from Hospital

Note: If the person who has experienced restored health is able, she/he may lead the Litany of thanks. If not, the leader may do so. This service may be concluded with refreshments and visiting.

Materials Needed
A Bible, candle

Preparation and Environment
Gather participants, with the person who is celebrating improved health or return from hospitalization, in a place of honor.

Introduction
(Light the candle and call the group to prayer.)
We rejoice in gratitude today that our friend N. has been restored to health and returned to us after her/his recent illness/hospitalization.

Opening Song *(appropriate song of thanks)*

Opening Prayer

Leader God of all gifts,
God who hears our prayer,
we come to you with hearts full of thanks
that N. has been restored to health,
and is once again a part of our community.
In gratitude we remember the stories of those whom Jesus healed,
of how they leaped, danced, rejoiced, and proclaimed your glory.
It is in their spirit of joy and gratitude that we come to you today.

Scripture Acclamation
Alleluia *(sung)*

Scripture
Mark 6:53–56

Scripture Response
Alleluia *(sung)*

Litany of Thanks

(Response after each invocation: "Thank you, Lord, for giving us life. Alleluia." It may be sung.)

Leader   Thank you, Gracious God, for all the gifts you have given me.

All   Thank you, Lord, for giving us life. Alleluia.

Leader   Thank you, Healing Lord, for rebuilding and restoring my body to health.

All   Thank you, Lord, for giving us life. Alleluia.

Leader   Thank you, healing Lord, for the marvels of medicine, the nurses and doctors who helped restore me to health.

All   Thank you, Lord, for giving us life. Alleluia.

Leader   Thank you, healing Lord, for all I received in my illness. For water that cooled me, for food that sustained me, for medication and those who treated me, for those who prayed and were concerned.

All   Thank you, Lord, for giving us life. Alleluia.

Leader   Thank you, healing Lord, for reuniting me to the flow of daily life and my friends and neighbors.

All   Thank you, Lord, for giving us life. Alleluia.

Leader   Thank you, healing Lord, the time you have allotted me, for the life you have offered me, and for the blessing of each new day.

All   Thank you, Lord, for giving us life. Alleluia.

Leader   Thank you, healing Lord, for being with me, for listening to me, and for taking me seriously.

All   Thank you, Lord, for giving us life. Alleluia.

Leader   Thank you, healing Lord, for receiving today's thank you.

All   Thank you, Lord, for giving us life. Alleluia.

Leader   Thank you, Lord, thank you very much.

All   Thank you, Lord, for giving us life. Alleluia.

Concluding Prayer

Leader   God of all Gifts, you have reunited N. to the flow of daily life with us, and for this we give you thanks and praise. May she/he by proper care, rest, and recreation, continue to be whole and healthy. May she/he, and we, be sensitive to those who are sick. May we be aware of their pain and respond to their needs of support and prayer. May our prayerful gratitude be shown in our own enjoyment of life, in our care, and in our own gift of good health. Blessed are you, Lord our God, who heals and saves your people.

All   Amen.

Closing Song
(appropriate song of thanks)

When a Resident Dies

Materials Needed
A Bible, a candle, a rose, printed copy of the Scripture passage to be used and a printed copy of the ritual, a Memory Book listing all who have died in the facility.

Preparation and Environment
Gather the participants in the deceased resident's room.

Gathering
Leader   We gather together today to remember N.
We gather here in the room she/he called home.
We gather to remember the presence of this special woman/man
    who shared the joys and sorrows of life with us.
We gather to remember how she/he was a role model
    for this Christian community.

Presentation of Symbols
Leader   *(Candle)* We light this candle, this symbol of Christ's light in a world sometimes filled with darkness. As it burns we remember the little pieces of light that N. brought to our lives.

Leader   *(Rose)* We place this rose on N.'s bed as a symbol of her/his presence. Let its beauty remind us of the personal gifts N. shared with us.

Leader   *(Memory Book)* We inscribe N.'s name into our Memory Book that we might not forget that she/he once touched our lives and remember her/him and her/his family in our thought and prayer.

Scripture Reading
A short passage that speaks to the life of the resident, was a favorite of the resident, or a passage from among the readings for Masses for the Dead: John 11 :5–26, Matthew 25:34, 2 Timothy 2:11–12. After proclaiming the Scripture passage, hang a copy of it on the door of the room.

We place this Scripture passage on the door. May all who pass this room recall that a faith-filled follower of Christ has returned to God.

Closing Prayer

Leader   Let us pray: Loving God, you are attentive to the voice of our pleading. Let us find in your Son, Jesus, comfort in our sadness, certainty in our doubt, and courage to live through the hours and days ahead. Make our faith strong through Christ our Lord. Amen.

(The Closing Prayer may also incorporate personal words or symbols of farewell. If the body is still present in the room, participants may be invited to trace a sign of the cross on the forehead or lips while praying their farewells.)

In Times of Sadness, Anxiety, Frustration, Doubt

Materials Needed
Bible, candle

Call to Prayer

Leader   When we are sad, fearful, anxious, frustrated or doubtful, God is with us calling us together to hear his word, and to find in each other hope, love, and the power of the Holy Spirit to help us take heart.

Musical Meditation
Something like "How Long, O Lord"*

Scripture
Isaiah 43:2–3

Responsorial Psalm
Psalm 139:1–18**

Leader   You search me, Lord, and know me.
Wherever I sit or stand,
you read my inmost thoughts;
whenever I walk or rest,
you know where I have been.

All   Yahweh, I know you are near.

Leader   Before a word slips from my tongue,
Lord, you know what I will say.
You close in on me,
pressing your hand upon me.
All this overwhelms me—
too much to understand!

All   Yahweh, I know you are near.

Leader   Where can I hide from you?
How can I escape your presence?
I scale the heavens, you are there!

*Dan Schutte, OCP Publications, 5536 NE Hassalo, Portland, OR 97213. Either a recorded or live rendition.
**"You Are Near" by Dan Schutte, OCP Publications, may also be used.

I plunge to the depths, you are there.

If I fly toward the dawn
or settle across the sea,
even there you take hold of me
your right hand directs me.

All   Yahweh, I know you are near.

Leader   If I think night will hide me
and darkness give me cover,
I find darkness is not dark.
For your night shines like day,
darkness and light are one.

All   Yahweh, I know you are near.

Leader   You created every part of me,
 knitting me in my mother's womb.
For such handiwork, I praise you.
Awesome this great wonder!
I see it so clearly!

All   Yahweh, I know you are near.

Leader   You watched every bone
taking shape in secret,
forming in the hidden depths.
You saw my body grow
according to your design.

All   Yahweh, I know you are near.

You recorded all my days
before they ever began.
How deep are your thoughts!
How vast their sum!
like countless grains of sand,
well beyond my grasp.

All   Yahweh, I know you are near.

Scripture

Luke 8:22–25

Homily/Intercessory Prayer

(Make this a kind of combined dialogue homily/intercessory prayer of the people. After a few words by the Leader, invite participants to share their fears, doubts, concerns.)

Introduction to Sharing

Leader O God, there are times when our doubts and anxieties and fears swirl around inside us with much turmoil. In those times we come to you for comfort. Let us pray: *(Pass a lighted candle to each person as they speak. After each prayer, all respond: "Be not afraid. God is near.")*

Concluding Prayer

Leader We gather all that has been shared and offer it to you, Loving God, in the words Jesus, your Son taught us. Our Father...

Concluding Song

"Be Not Afraid"*

*Bob Dufford, OCP Publications

When Concerned for Family or Friends

Materials Needed
Votive, or tea lights, matches, small sheets of paper and pens, a small basket.

Introduction and Preparation
Invite participants, if they are able, to write their concerns for family and friends on the small sheets of paper. If they are not able, have volunteers help write their concerns.

Opening Prayer
Leader   Loving God, we gather here today to remember those family members and friends for whom we are concerned. We come with our requests to you and ask that you hear our prayer.

Presentation of Prayer and Lighting of Candles
(Participants are invited to place the written message in the basket, articulate their prayer, leave a coin and light a candle.)

Response After Each Prayer: "Lord, hear our prayer."

Concluding Prayer
Leader   Gracious God, we know you hear our prayer and are grateful for your compassion. Watch over, with care, those for whom we pray. Gathering our prayers together, let us pray the prayer Jesus taught us: Our Father...

On the Death of an Adult Child

Note: Before scheduling and celebrating this service, it would be advisable to meet with the resident who has lost an adult child. Suggest the possibility of the service and get their approval. Spend some time talking with the resident about memories they have of the child who has died. This service can also be adapted for use on the occasion of the death of a spouse.

Materials Needed
Photos of the child who has died (if possible, photos from various stages of the child's life), a small green plant, a candle.

Preparation and Environment
Inform residents and staff of their friend's loss and invite those who wish to join in supportive prayer. Gather the participants around a table on which the above materials have been arranged.

Introduction
Leader Our friend N. has lost her/his son/daughter. News of this type often comes as a shock. We seldom think that our children will die before us, who are older. And so, we gather in prayer and support of N. in her/his sorrow at this time.

Opening Prayer
Leader Gracious God, we have learned of the death of N., daughter/son of N. The news carries with it the shadow of sorrow and fear, for it reminds us that, someday, we, too, shall die. It also carries with it the shadow of grief, for at our age, we feel that we should die before our children. But your ways are not ours, God. And so we gather here today to remember with N. her/his child and to pray with and for her/him and the members of her/his family in their time of sorrow.

All Lord, may the news of this death be for us a holy message. Let us be grateful for life today. Let us not waste our days, or be unprepared for the arrival of our own death.

Story Sharing
Leader Lord of life and death, today we remember the death of N. child of N. We pause now to recall the good times N. and her/his child shared together.

(Invite the person who has lost a child to share pleasant stories about the child. Use the photos and your previous conversation with the resident to help trigger reminiscences. After each story, all might respond: "Glory to God for a good life.")

Litany of Thanks

Leader For all that has been in the life of our dearly departed N., let us pray:

All We thank you, Lord.

Leader In gratitude for the treasures just shared,

All We thank you, Lord.

Leader For all that was enjoyed by N's. family and friends,

All We thank you, Lord.

Leader For humor and work,

All We thank you, Lord.

Leader For affection and trust,

All We thank you, Lord.

Leader For memories of good times,

All We thank you, Lord.

Leader For love that is beyond the touch of death,

All We thank you, Lord.

Leader For the presence we feel of N. today,

All We thank you, Lord.

Leader For the support of family and friends at this time,

All We thank you, Lord.

Leader For our belief in resurrection,

All We thank you, Lord.

Concluding Prayer

Leader Mysterious Lord of Life and Death,

a special part of N.'s life has died.
Send to her/him your angel of consolation,
    for we know her/his sorrow is heavy and deep.
Mary, Mother of Sorrows,
    who was also a parent who lost an adult child,
    you know the pain of such loss.
Be a comfort to N. in this time of sorrow.

Loving God and Merciful Mary, support N.
    wrap her/him in your gentle love
    as she/he attempts to carry this bitter cross,
    just as your Son, Jesus, carried his cross.
His cross led to Resurrection and New Life
    which is also waiting for N., child of N.

Ritual Action

As a sign of our belief that N's child lives on in her/his memory and lives now with Christ, we present to N. this green plant.
(The small green plant is presented to the parent along with a copy of the above prayer signed by residents and staff.)

In Thanksgiving for Good News

This prayer can be used for any communal or personal "good news" occasion. Personal good news might include the birth of a grandchild or great-grandchild, a family wedding, especially if the resident is not able to attend, the renewed health of a family member, etc.

Materials Needed

Any symbol related to the occasion (photos, newspaper clippings, letters, announcement cards, etc.)

Introduction

We gather today to give thanks to God for the good news of _____. *(Dialogue with participants about the good news. If it is personal good news invite the person experiencing the news to tell the group about it.)*

Prayer

(All respond: "Thank you, Lord" after each invocation.)

Leader   Loving God, we praise you and are filled with gratitude
for the numerous gifts,
the countless blessings, that come to us from you.

All   Thank you, Lord.

Leader   Your blessings come in times of joy,
in times of success, in times of honor,
in times of birth, in times of renewed health,
and always as life-giving.

All   Thank you, Lord.

Leader   We thank you, God of Gifts,
for friendships, family, and fun,
for the care, compassion, and generosity of others,
and for your great gift of life.

All   Thank you, Lord.

Leader   Gracious God, we thank you for all the gifts

that flow day and night
into our lives.

All   Thank you, Lord.

Leader   Today, with full hearts,
in the company of Jesus, Mary,
and all your saints,
we praise you for the good that has come to us.

All   Thank you, Lord.

Leader   Praise be to you, Lord our God,
in your bountiful love,
you bless us with good things.

All   Thank you, Lord.

Concluding Song
(appropriate song of thanks)

Gesture of Friendship
Appropriate gestures of congratulations for personal good news. Share a "fun" food treat: sundaes, milk shakes, root beer floats, etc.